All-Color Guide

Gems

and Jewelry
BY JOEL AREM

A Ridge Press Book

BANTAM BOOKS
TORONTO · NEW YORK · LONDON · SYDNEY

Photo Credits

Joel Arem—all photographs except the following
De Beers: 42;
General Electric Company: 134,135;
Gemological Institute of America: 7 (btm. rt.), 35, 36, 43, 111 (btm. rt.);
K. Mikimoto & Company, Ltd.: 90;
Prado Museum, Madrid: 9 (left);
Scala, New York/Florence: 10;
Union Carbide Corporation: 133, 136;
Universal Diamond Industries: 143, 145.

Acknowledgments: A & S Gem & Mineral Co., Lazare Kaplan International, Goldberg-Weiss, Harry Winston, N. W Ayer, John Van Itallie, A. E. Goldstein, Pete J. Dunn, Gemological Institute of America, Casper Beesley, William Huff, Chatham Created Gems, Inc., Universal Diamond Industries, General Electric Company, Joseph Koach.

Special thanks to Karen L. Johnson
Front Cover: Turquoise set in Silver superimposed on Sphalerite
Back Cover: Emerald and Diamond Ring
Title Page: top left, Strontium Titanate in Gold ring; top right, Rhodochrosite; bottom, Tourmaline

---

GEMS AND JEWELRY

A Bantam Book published by arrangement with The Ridge Press, Inc.
Bantam edition / 6 printings through April 1983.
Designed and produced by The Ridge Press, Inc. All rights reserved.
Copyright© 1975 in all countries of the International Copyright Union
by The Ridge Press, Inc. This book may not be reproduced in whole
or in part by mimeograph or any other means, without permission.
For information address: The Ridge Press, Inc., 25 West 43rd Street,
New York, N.Y. 10036.

D. L. TO: 1634 -1984

ISBN: 0-553-25140-6

Library of Congress Catalog Card Number: 75-10948
Published simultaneously in the United States and Canada.

Bantam Books are published by Bantam Books, Inc.
Its trademark, consisting of the words "Bantam Books" and the portrayal
of a rooster, is Registered in U.S. Patent and Trademark Office
and other countries. Marca Registrada.

Bantam Books, Inc., 666 Fifth Avenue, New York, N.Y. 10103.
Printed in Spain by Artes Gráficas Toledo, S.A.
15   14   13   12   11   10   9   8   7   6

Contents

Introduction

A very thin slice of gabbro, an igneous rock from Point Sal, California, reveals details of the rock's history.

Introduction

Gems are among the most fascinating and exciting of objects. They have intrigued mankind since before the dawn of recorded history. Even today nothing creates quite as effective an image of pure, tangible, *concentrated* value as a box overflowing with jewels.

This mystique is unrivaled among the commodities held precious by mankind. The fact that the mystique exists is seldom questioned, but its nature is harder to determine. Basically, the entire lore, history, and value of gems is based on the combination of beauty and utility they possess. Man has a deep-seated need to create artistic works and to adorn himself. Although many kinds of natural materials, such as mineral pigments, can be applied to this end, gems occupy a special place. Jewels are found among the remains of most human civilizations, and tell us as much about their creators in some cases as pottery, clothing, and tools.

The high value placed on gems since earliest times is due to their unique properties. The colors of gem materials are among the richest and purest in nature. For example, the depth and purity of emerald's green hue inspired reverence in Pre-Columbian societies, and large emeralds became objects of worship. Gems are also hard and durable. It is easy to see how man, with his short life span and vulnerability to nature's forces, must have regarded such "indestructible" and permanent objects with awe. Man's embellishment of gemological properties led to a wealth of superstitious belief so strong and pervasive that its remnants are with us even today.

Gem value is based on such properties as beauty, durability, and rarity, as well as the fashion of the times. These criteria have become well established over a period of many centuries. Most gems are mined and can be regarded as mineral resources. Just as in the case of gold mines and oil wells, the supply in any one place eventually runs out. This adds a "collector value" to gems from specific mines that may now be exhausted. But gems represent a tiny percentage of the vast tonnage of minerals mined yearly. Their scarcity is a fundamental fact of geochemistry and the operation of laws of chance.

In inflationary periods throughout history, commodities that have intrinsic value have been greatly prized. Gold, silver, and other precious metals have such value, because they have universal acceptance as a medium of exchange. Antiques, rare coins, works of art, and other objects may have collector value, which implies acceptance as value objects by a limited group of people. Gemstones, especially diamonds, have attributes that place them in both categories.

The historical record of gems indicates a strong level of general

Gems are usually cut from crystals, such as this tourmaline (opp. l.). Sometimes cut tourmalines display several color zones (top r.). Sharpest and loveliest "eye" of any gem: cat's-eye chrysoberyl (btm. r.).

acceptance, akin to that reserved for the precious metals. Fashion might cause temporary rises and dips in the market value of particular gem varieties, but gemstones in general have proven to be time-honored means of storing value. And few other commodities allow a person to store as much value in as small a space.

Modern technology has enabled man to duplicate in the laboratory many of nature's masterpieces. Gemstone synthesis is one of the great achievements of the 20th Century. Today one can buy man-made ruby, emerald, sapphire, spinel, alexandrite, and other gems, and more gem varieties are sure to be manufactured in the future. Gem identification and authentication has taken on new dimensions and become quite complex. Yet the difference in value between a natural and synthetic gem can be enormous. For example, a ten-carat synthetic and natural ruby might differ in value by as much as $50,000. This sum is large enough to make it imperative that a means of distinguishing natural and synthetic gemstones be developed.

All these factors combine to produce a difficult situation for the average gem buyer. The complexity in the grading and evaluation of gems seems mysterious. The intricacies of the gem trade are intimidating. And the large dollar values involved can sometimes make buying jewelry appear to be an expedition into financially perilous territory, fraught with hidden obstacles and traps.

Yet the basic factors that determine gem value are easy to under-

stand. Few gem varieties are likely to be encountered in a typical shop. Appraising a gem is a fairly straightforward procedure, although the end result is definitely a measure of the experience of the appraiser.

To the eye, natural and synthetic gems may appear identical. The gem buyer will probably not be able to distinguish them, but he can at least be aware of which synthetics exist and what kinds of imitations are being sold widely. More now than ever before, a compendium of basic information in the hands of the jewelry buyer is vitally needed. That is why this book has been written.

Gems and Jewelry is consumer-oriented. Its main purpose is to present an overview of the entire field of gemstones and to provide enough guidelines to make the display in a typical jewelry shop familiar and comprehensible. Throughout the book an attempt is made to provide practical information and tips on judging quality. There is extensive information on the valuation and marketing of gemstones, current market practices, tradenames, and labeling policies and regulations.

This is not a technical book. Rather, it is written as an introductory guide. It contains enough information to be of practical value to both jewelers and consumers. But the main purpose of the book will be fulfilled if it helps people find a visit to a jewelry shop a pleasurable and worthwhile excursion in familiar surroundings.

Gem History

Gems were probably used by primitive man in connection with mystical rites. The vibrant colors, transparency, and unusual forms of naturally occurring gem materials are all capable of inspiring awe in superstitious cultures. For example, quartz crystals or flattened and stream-polished pebbles were used thousands of years ago for starting fires by concentrating the rays of the sun. Such objects must have been regarded as wellsprings of great and mysterious powers. Yet these same materials were also prized for their beauty and thus served as ornaments. Various prehistoric cultures therefore regarded gems as objects of either religion or adornment.

Closely related to mysticism was primitive medicine, and here too gems played a major role. The wearing of amulets was practiced in the early days of Egyptian civilization. Such objects are ornaments inscribed with "magic" symbols to ward off evil spirits or aid the wearer. The production of such baubles may well have been the earliest form of lapidary, or gem-cutting art. The first jewelry items were probably beads—pebbles drilled and crudely strung as necklaces, or worn as pendants and bracelets. Later in history beads would be more perfectly polished, and/or inscribed with symbolic markings.

Such amulets, covered with images and religious symbols, were common in ancient Babylonia, Persia, and Assyria, where they were

known as cylinders. Over a period of centuries the carving of gem materials developed into a great art. This can be traced through the production of beetle-images called scarabs, prominent in Egyptian culture, and culminating in the exquisite artistry and great craftsmanship of the lapidaries of Persia, Greece, and Rome. The beetle represented the immortality of the soul and became a dominant symbol in Egyptian art during the 9th Dynasty, about 2050 B.C.

Thus, by the time of Christ, some gem trade routes were already well established in the civilized world. This is proved by the discovery of lapis lazuli and emerald ornaments in Egyptian tombs. Lapis was imported from Turkestan into Egypt nearly ten centuries before Moses led the Hebrews out of bondage. Lapis, a beautiful blue gem that was probably called sapphire in ancient times, came from Badakshan in Afghanistan, then called Media. These are the oldest operating mines known, having produced steadily for 7,000 years. The mining of turquoise in the Sinai Peninsula is of similar antiquity.

It is not too surprising, then, that the King James version of the Bible contains more than 1,700 references to gems, under nearly 125 Greek and Hebrew names. These names are a mass of confusion. In the absence of definitive gem-testing methods, ancient societies relied on color as a guide. Individual gems that occur in various colors thus acquired a rich variety of names, many of which have persisted even into modern times. Confusion also arises in the translation of ancient writings into modern language. In some cases there is no definitive way **9**

Portrait of Spain's Queen Isabella (l.) reveals the prominence of gems in royal fashion. Diamond mining in Africa (r.), now highly mechanized, was once the job of laborers.

of assigning a particular modern gem name to a word used thousands of years ago.

The specific uses of gems have varied in different historical periods. In the Greek and Roman periods, carving attained the state of great art, including the introduction of the cameo, or raised relief technique, around 300 B.C. In ancient Rome pearls were highly esteemed. Julius Caesar is reputed to have paid the modern equivalent of $300,000 for a single fine pearl! But opals and other gems were also prized, and wealthy Romans tried to outdo each other in acquiring fine stones.

In the centuries that followed the fall of the Roman Empire gems re-established themselves as objects of magical powers. For example, the signs of the zodiac were associated with specific gems. The number 12 is of great significance in this context. Each of the 12 tribes of ancient Israel had been represented by a gem in the breastplate of the High Priest. Centuries later, each of the 12 apostles was assigned a specific gemstone, and the same for the 12 months of the year. The idea of birthstones appears to have come along much later—probably the 18th Century.

In the Middle Ages, the Church dominated the thinking of European man, and gems became part of holy rituals. Sapphire acquired status as the favorite ringstone of high Church officials. Chalices set with precious stones became artistic treasures. Further mysticism embellished the already large heritage of magical powers associated with gemstones, and gems became tools in medical practice. The curative powers ascribed to certain gems were incredible. Doubtless sometimes a cure was effected, since psychosomatic illness can be cured as easily with a sugar pill as with swallowed gem powders.

In the 17th and 18th Centuries, scholars began to seriously study the glittering creations of nature we call minerals. With the development of the science of mineralogy came greater knowledge of gems, and the science of gemology was born. Scientific tests were developed for recognizing gems and distinguishing one from another. Gradually the

complex nomenclature of previous centuries was sorted out, and the world entered the modern age of gems. By the middle of the 19th Century, gems for adornment were in full vogue, and the Romantic era was marked by tremendous creativity and artistry that swept through all fields, including jewelry. In 1868, diamonds from South Africa were first sold in Paris. Thus began a century of passion for "girl's best friend" that continues to the present time. Developments in jewelry design allowed the production of standardized settings, thus revolutionizing the jewelry market before 1900.

The 20th Century has witnessed tides of fashion in all fields, including jewelry. Different gems have been in vogue in different decades, but in recent years worldwide affluence has reached such high levels that fine gems are in great demand. Gem synthesis has now made it possible for even a modest purse to afford stones that rival the world's finest in appearance.

What Are Gems?

Gemstones are minerals, the fundamental building blocks of the earth. A mineral is a naturally occurring inorganic chemical element or compound, with a definite crystal structure and a composition that varies within defined limits.

Not all minerals are useful as gems. Since gems must be visually attractive, only minerals with ornamental qualities are suitable. This criterion reduces the total available catalog of about 2,400 mineral species to approximately 100 that have been cut into gemstones.

Some materials of biological origin are also used as gems. These include amber, coral, pearl, shells, and jet, a hard variety of coal. Organic gems lack the durability and hardness of many minerals, but **11**

Most gems are minerals, usually brightly colored species, such as this wulfenite (above) from Theba, Arizona. Brilliant goldcrown (opp.) is shown in The Virgin of Chancellor Rolin *by Jan van Eyck.*

have been highly valued because of their beauty and scarcity.

With this in mind we may define some basic and often confusing terms. Gemstones are minerals with high ornamental value. Gems are the beautiful objects cut from such materials. A jewel is either a gem or an artistic creation incorporating precious metals in which gems may be set. A fine pearl is considered a gem. Other organic substances could be called gem materials.

In the past the terms "precious" and "semi-precious" have been widely used. Today their use creates confusion, because a poor diamond can be worth less than a very fine and rare variety of garnet. Since there is no particular advantage in their use, both terms should be completely abandoned.

In the Grand Canyon,
Arizona (opp.),
we can see the results
of natural forces of erosion.
Earth pressures cause
banding in rocks such
as this schist (l.)

Strange as it seems, the history of our civilization is intimately linked to the existence of pretty bits of mineral and organic material. Gems have been used as symbols of wealth, as talismans, as objects of worship, as money, and as medicine. They have been made into jewelry, used as personal adornment, and have served as investments and storehouses of wealth. Wars have been waged over gems. Violent crimes have been committed in their pursuit. Kingdoms have been overthrown and part of the globe explored and mapped to obtain them. Few commodities have achieved the level of importance in world affairs reserved for gems.

Gem Criteria

Hardness is a major factor. If a gem is too soft it will scratch easily and, if worn, its beauty would be rapidly lost due to abrasion. Some extremely soft minerals are cut for collectors and can be thought of as non-commercial gems. But their lack of durability makes it questionable if the term "gem" can be applied to them. Durability combines various characteristics into a general term that indicates how well a gem wears in daily use. Objects such as pearls are not too hard, but hold up well and retain their beauty for a long time.

Rarity is a major factor in evaluating a gem, for much of a gem's value comes from its scarcity. The material itself might be very uncommon. On the other hand, the rarity of a particular gem might be due to its large size compared to most other gems of the same material, or its extremely fine or unusual color.

Color is of paramount importance in a gem. It can make the difference between $10 and $10,000 per carat in some gemstones. The range of color to be found in the mineral kingdom is enormous, and there is great subtlety in the variation of color in a single mineral species. Some minerals occur in a wide range of colors, such as tourmaline, beryl, quartz, and spinel. In this case value is directly linked to the fashion of the times—that is, what color is considered "most desirable."

Brilliance and **dispersion** affect gem value, especially in the case of colorless materials. Brilliance is the effect produced by the return of **13**

light from the gem to the eye, and is largely a function of proper cutting. Dispersion is the optical phenomenon that creates the color play in diamond. High dispersion is found in only a few stones, but in these it is responsible for an unusual degree of beauty. Usually brilliance is sacrificed to some degree when a stone is cut for maximum dispersion, or vice versa. Optimum cutting would maximize both qualities, hence the search for a set of "ideal" proportions for cutting diamonds.

Clarity, or freedom from flaws, largely determines value in the case of faceted gems. In past times flawed stones were considered attractive, but today's fashion associates high value with complete absence of inclusions or flaws. Since most minerals acquire such internal imperfections as a normal part of the growth process, completely flawless or "clean" gems are extremely scarce in many species. In Colombian emerald and Burmese ruby, for example, such perfection is almost unknown. Even nearly flawless gems of such materials are in great demand and command a high price. In the case of quartz and topaz, on the other hand, large transparent and clean gems are frequently cut.

Transparency is the absence of "cloudiness" or "milkiness" that would scatter light entering a gem. A faceted gemstone may be free of inclusions or flaws visible to the naked eye, but might contain thousands of tiny bubbles or mineral inclusions that could be resolved only under high magnification. Examples are the bubbles in white quartz and the "silk" in star sapphires.

Beauty is the most important criterion of all. It depends, of course, on the judgment of the observer and is thus almost totally subjective. But more significant is the fact that what is generally considered beautiful or desirable may change with time, and vary from one culture to another. The value of gems is thus intimately linked to fashion, and the vogue of the time.

Portability is a less obvious but very important aspect of gem value. You can close your fist around a diamond worth several million dollars. Only a gem can offer this degree of high value captured in a small space. Many a fortune has been saved because its owner could escape economic or political upheaval carrying his gem hoard easily concealed on his or her person.

Few gems display in perfection all of the above criteria, and even the criteria themselves have modifying factors. For instance, a dark color might be desirable in a green tourmaline, but if the color is *too* dark the gem actually may lose value. A large gem might be far more valuable than a smaller one, but the larger stone might be less saleable because of its higher cost. A gem may possess great value because of its scarcity. But if the gem is so scarce that few people have ever heard of it, its **14** marketability, and hence its value, may be less than expected.

Origin of Gems

The earth is a gigantic chemical factory, within which all the chemical elements are mixed and combined. Minerals are naturally occurring chemical compounds and elements. Every mineral is characterized by a definite crystal structure and a chemical composition that varies within defined limits. A rock is made up of one or more minerals. Rocks are classified according to the minerals they contain and the process of their formation. Igneous rocks form when molten material cools and solidifies, either at depth or at or near the earth's surface. Sedimentary rocks form at the earth's surface. They consist of the remains of marine organisms that settled and deposited in an ocean or lake, or the compacted and solidified debris of rocks exposed to the erosional forces of wind, water, and ice. Such erosional fragments are called sediments. Metamorphic rocks are formed when enormous compressional forces, sometimes accompanied by heat, crush, deform, and alter pre-existing rocks of various kinds. Such forces are due to movement in the earth's crust, and the rock alteration process is called metamorphism.

Specific types of minerals and gems are associated with specific rock types. A knowledge of rocks is essential in prospecting for minerals. Quartz, for example, is extremely common. It even makes up most beach sands! But *gem* quartz occurs only in limited geologic environments. The gem-mining areas of the world are limited in number. The most important sources of the world's colored gemstones are in sedimentary deposits, such as gravel beds. Next in importance is the pegmatite dike, a special type of igneous body in which large crystals may form. Some gems also form in metamorphic rocks, especially marbles. Accurate production statistics are available on diamonds, but not for colored stones. Most gem mines are small compared to diamond mines, and some are worked only when demand creates high enough prices for the gems they yield. These factors prevent a "flood" of colored gems from entering world markets at one time.

Marketing of Gemstones

Gemstones are found on nearly every continent of the world. With few exceptions gem occurrences are in remote areas, and considerable effort is required to bring them to the marketplace. The various stages in this enterprise all add their share to the eventual cost of cut gems.

Gems pass through many hands between mine and marketplace. In many parts of the world gem crystals are found by local miners who may or may not be aware of their ultimate market value. These rough gems may be sold to local entrepreneurs who start the stones on their way to the retailer. Some of these men are well-educated professionals who have found a niche with high profit potential, but their business is loaded with pitfalls. Gem rough is extremely difficult to evaluate. The **15**

trained eye of a buyer must be able to spot flaws that affect gem value and decide if they can be eliminated by careful cutting. The size of gem rough determines its value, so the buyer must also be able to determine the sizes of the gems that the rough will yield. The color of the cut stones must be extrapolated from the appearance of the rough. Obviously, errors in judgment can be very costly at this stage, and some of the cost of mistakes must be added to the eventual price of the good gems that are recovered.

Gemstone deposits are sometimes profitably worked by hand sorting, whereas mechanized mining would not be cost effective. Good examples of this are the opal fields of Australia and, when active, the Burmese gravels. The slower hand methods also insure that the gem deposits will yield their treasures gradually, and thus be productive over a longer period of time.

Normally gemstones from the mines are sold either to exporters or to cutters. In recent years there has been a trend in most gem-producing countries to cut all fine gems locally.

Rough or cut gems are exported from the country of origin to importers in other lands. The actual number of middlemen varies tremendously. Some companies travel the world buying gem rough at the source, bring the rough back to their own shops for cutting, and then sell the cut stones at wholesale or retail. Other companies buy rough from importers and cut it themselves or in other shops. Sometimes, where local labor costs are high (as in the United States) it is expedient to import rough, send it to another country for cutting, and then import the cut gems. With the exception of diamond, there is no standard pattern in

16

Consumers are aware of gems through the jewelry trade (l.). Some stores specialize in the widest possible variety of gem materials (A&S Gem and Mineral Co., New York, r.)

the gem trade, or for any particular type of stone. The flow of rough and cut material may change rapidly with market conditions.

The grading of gem material is a major factor in sales on all levels. Not all the material, rough or cut, from any particular source is of the same quality. The ability of a merchant to accurately appraise the market value of a parcel of stones determines his profit or loss. The range of value of finished stones, even from a single parcel of rough, can be enormous. Large stones are proportionally far more valuable, per carat, than smaller gems, even of the same quality.

A major role in the jewelry industry is played by the manufacturing jeweler. Seldom encountered at the retail level, this specialist acquires loose gems and sets them in gold and platinum settings, often with small diamonds. Other manufacturers deal only in metal items, such as charms and bracelets. Still others manufacture castings of various jewelry items, in which stones may be set. The services of the manufacturing jeweler make it possible for the retailer to select ready-to-wear items from catalogs, thus simplifying his job and enabling him to stock a wide variety of jewelry items he could not make himself.

When a stone appears in a retail shop it thus has built into its price such factors as the cost of rough, quality range of rough material, import and export duties, number of middlemen and their expertise, cost of cutting, and various other miscellaneous expenses. But perhaps the most significant contribution to retail costs is that of inventory. To provide a selection for his customers, the jeweler must tie up large sums of money in stock. The cost of maintaining this inventory can be extremely high, and is usually passed along to the customer in the price of jewelry items. But the trade-off value to the customer is the ability to see and select from a wide variety of jewelry pieces featuring many different gemstones.

Units of Measurement

The basic unit for weighing gemstones is the carat. This is defined as $^1/_5$ of a gram, and is not to be confused with the term "karat" used to describe the fineness of gold. Originally gems were compared in weight with the seeds of various plants, such as barley grain and the seeds of locust trees. The word "carat" may derive from the Greek word "keration." At the time of the emperor Constantine 24 kerations made up a golden solidus. Since pure gold is, by definition, 24 karat, the words "carat" and "karat" may thus be related in antiquity.

Since different seeds were used to weigh gems in various locations, there was no universal standard until 1907. In that year the International Committee on Weights and Measures proposed the so-called "metric carat" of $^1/_5$ gram. This unit was adopted in the United States in 1913 and various other countries between 1908 and 1930. There are 28.3 **17**

2.58mm	3.25mm	4.1mm	5.15mm	6.5mm	7.4mm
1/16 carat	1/8 carat	1/4 carat	1/2 carat	1 carat	1 1/2 carats

grams in an ounce, so a carat is equivalent to about .035 of an ounce. By comparison, a United States copper penny weighs about 15½ carats.

The carat is subdivided for convenience into 100 units called points. A gem weight would be expressed decimally as, for example, 11.36 carats, equivalent to 11 carats plus 36 points.

For pearls, the unit of weight is the grain. There are four grains in a carat. The price of pearls is calculated by a formula that involves the weight and a so-called "base price." The base price or base rate is affected by both size,and quality, and whether the pricing is for matched pearls. Today pearls are also measured in terms of diameter, expressed in millimeters. A millimeter is about .04 of an inch in length; a United States penny, for example, measures 19mm in diameter. A pearl weighing six grains is approximately 6mm in diameter.

Faceted and cabochon-cut gemstones are also measured in millimeters, as well as carats. Millimeter sizes are most often applied to synthetic and lower-priced stones, but any good appraisal of a gem would include both a weight and dimensions in the description. Jewelry mountings are manufactured to fit standard, or calibrated stones. Because such mountings are mass-produced and less costly than custom-made settings, it is easier and less expensive to set a calibrated stone than a free-size. Therefore, with less expensive gem materials, calibrated stones command a slightly higher price than random-sized gems. Finer gems are usually cut to conserve weight.

Rough gem materials may be weighed in carats, if the value of the rough is high; or in grams, ounces, or pounds for successively less-expensive material.

The following are carat weights of some commonly encountered objects, to form a basis for comparison and establish familiarity.

Copper paper clip: 2.9 cts.	United States dime (post-1965): 11.25 cts.
Office-size staple: 17 points	United States quarter (post-1965): 28.35 cts.

Gemstone Properties

We know the world around us by means of our senses. Every object has certain physical and chemical properties by which it can be identified. Some of these properties, such as "beauty," are completely subjective.

8.2mm 2 carats	9.35mm 3 carats	10.3mm 4 carats	11.1mm 5 carats	11.75mm 6 carats	12.4mm 7 carats

Others are measurable by various techniques. Modern chemistry is sophisticated and precise, but usually beyond the capabilities of the jeweler. The practical retailer, who may not have a chemical laboratory at his disposal, must therefore rely on various optical and physical properties for identification and evaluation.

Most gems are minerals, which are crystalline substances. In all solids the constituent atoms are arranged in geometric arrays, like a kind of three-dimensional wallpaper pattern. The atoms have fixed positions relative to one another, resulting in an internal regularity that affects the external shape of crystals, as well as their properties.

The atoms in crystals are held together by strong electrical forces called bonds. The bond strength within a solid varies with direction, somewhat like the grain of a plank of wood. A pine board may split easily along the grain, but will break irregularly, if at all, across the grain. In crystals, planes of weak bonds are directions of cleavage, or easy splitting. The way a crystal breaks is thus diagnostic of its internal atomic arrangement and is useful in identification.

Inclusions in gemstones are also sometimes diagnostic, not only of identity, but also of country of origin. Inclusions are foreign materials incorporated in a crystal at the time of growth. In the case of emeralds they can actually indicate the specific mine from which a crystal came. Many of the properties used in identification by the gemologist also affect the value of cut gems.

19

*Cleavage (above),
well displayed by mica, is a
basic property of solids.*

Color

Color is the most obvious feature of a gem, and the most critical in assessing gem value.

The color of any material is due to the nature of light itself, which may be thought of as a wave motion of energy. The basic unit in measuring waves is the distance between successive crests or troughs, called the wavelength. Different colors of light are merely different wavelengths. So-called "white light," such as sunlight, is a mixture of all the visible wavelengths. But when this light passes through a material, some wavelengths may be selectively absorbed. The remaining light that reaches our eyes is white light *minus* the absorbed colors. A ruby, for example, appears red because it absorbs blue, yellow, and green wavelengths. The longer the path through the material, the more absorption that occurs. So larger or thicker gems usually appear darker and richer in color than smaller stones. A colorless stone absorbs no wavelengths and allows white light to emerge unchanged.

Minerals acquire their color through several different processes. Some are idiochromatic, or "self-colored," meaning that their colors are inherent in the chemical and physical makeup of the materials themselves. For example, azurite is always blue and malachite is always some shade of green. Other minerals are allochromatic, or "other-colored," meaning that their colors are acquired through contamination by chemical impurities. For example, pure beryl is colorless. The presence of a trace of chromium turns it green (emerald); iron impurities color beryl blue-green or blue (aquamarine). Combinations of such impurities create a wide range of colors in various gemstones.

For the idiochromatic minerals, consistency makes color a useful identifying feature. But for other minerals that can be colored by various chemical impurities, color can be a very misleading and unreliable characteristic. For the gem buyer this problem is compounded by the limited range of colors exhibited by the commercially popular stones found in most jewelry shops. To most people garnet is a red gem, yet it occurs in shades of purple, orange, pink, yellow, and green. Jade is not only green, but can be blue, purple, red, brown, gray, white, or yellow. In gems, subtleties of color can mean enormous differences in value.

For most gemstones, depth of color and richness of color are synonymous with higher value. This is especially apparent in the case of topaz, aquamarine, and amethyst. But too dark a gem color can actually detract from its value, as in the case of green tourmaline, blue sapphire, and even some emeralds. Certain colors in some gems are highly prized, as in the rare pinkish-orange sapphire known as padparadscha, and purple or blue jade.

The light in which gems are viewed is obviously important. Sunlight contains a well-balanced mixture of wavelengths, but can sometimes be so bright that colors are "washed out." Incandescent lamps give a light that is warm and yellowish-red, while fluorescent lamps tend to be bluish. A good illumination for displaying gems is a balanced mixture of fluorescent and incandescent light.

Some materials exhibit different colors in different directions, because of differential absorption characteristics. Gems that show two different colors are called dichroic, illustrated by tourmaline and cordierite. Those that display three colors, such as tanzanite and spodumene, are called trichroic. A cut stone may appear one or another of these colors, depending how the rough is oriented with respect to the table, or flat top of the gem.

Tenacity and Hardness

The way a mineral breaks is largely dependent on the bonds holding its atoms together. If planes of weakness (cleavage planes) exist between layers of atoms, the mineral will tend to split along these planes. If no such planes exist, breakage tends to be irregular and is termed fracture. The resistance that a substance offers to breakage or chipping is called tenacity.

Irregular breakage in minerals is described as fibrous, splintery, hackly, even, uneven, or conchoidal. The latter resembles the surface of a beach shell, with concentric curved lines. The word "conchoidal" itself means "shell form," and this fracture is seen commonly on glass and quartz.

Cleavage is ranked as perfect, good, fair, or poor. Nearly all minerals display fracture, but not all minerals have cleavage. A less-pronounced tendency for splitting to occur along planes is called parting. Minerals with good cleavage make poor ringstones, because they may split if struck a sharp blow. Minerals with good cleavage are also difficult to cut.

"Toughness" is another way of describing tenacity. Tough stones, such as jade, wear extremely well and can be carved into thin and delicate shapes without breaking.

The hardness of a material can be determined by scratching. In this case a hard rock is drawn against a soft plate of gypsum, producing a deep furrow.

Hardness is not a measure of fragility, but rather of resistance to scratching. The assessment of hardness varies with the measurement technique used. All minerals can be ranked in order of relative scratchability. One can scratch various minerals against each other, and arrange them in sequence of increasing hardness. On a simple scale of 1 to 10, with 10 the hardest, any mineral would scratch any other mineral with a lower hardness number. Such an experiment was first done by an Austrian mineralogist, Friedrich Mohs, who picked ten common minerals to represent the division points of the scale. The Mohs scale has survived the decades since its inception and is widely used today:

1. Talc	6. Orthoclase	For reference:	
2. Gypsum	7. Quartz	2½	Fingernail
3. Calcite	8. Topaz	3–4	Copper penny
4. Fluorite	9. Corundum	5½	Knife blade
5. Apatite	10. Diamond	5½	Window glass

It should be noted that while diamond is the hardest known substance, and will therefore scratch any other substance, it is also somewhat brittle and can be shattered or split. This is perhaps the best example of the difference between hardness and tenacity. In some directions in diamond, the atomic bonds are extremely strong, creating great hardness. In other directions, the bonds are relatively weak, and so diamond has perfect cleavage.

For use as a gemstone, a mineral should ideally have both great hardness and tenacity. A brittle substance may chip badly with wear, and ultimately slip out of a setting. Even the act of setting a fragile gem may cause it to break. Relatively soft gems may show signs of wear after a short time, because they are easily scratched by debris in the air that accumulates and rubs against them. Eventually the surfaces of such a stone are so worn that brilliance and transparency are lost, and repolishing is necessary.

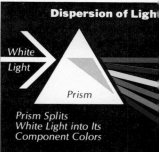

Dispersion of Light

White Light

Prism

Prism Splits White Light into Its Component Colors

Hardness tests are never performed on faceted gems because of the risk of damage. Hardness is used more frequently in testing rough and opaque gems, where a scratch on the back will not be visible.

Refraction

Light travels through space at a constant speed of about 186,000 miles per second. It is not slowed down very much by air, but in solids and liquids it is both slowed and forced to change its path. The degree to which light is slowed down in a material, relative to air, is called the index of refraction of the material. This index is also a measure of the bending of light in a solid or liquid medium. Gems cut from highly refractive materials tend to be brilliant and bright, and this factor sometimes affects the style of cutting of particular gems.

Light traveling in different directions through certain minerals is bent to a different degree. This difference in refractive index can be so extreme that the back facets of a gemstone may appear to be "doubled" as seen through the body of the stone. The refractive indices for most gems are constant and useful in identification. An instrument devised to rapidly determine the refractive indices of a gem is called the gem refractometer.

Some types of gems display only one refractive index. Others display two or three, depending on fundamental differences in crystalline structure of these various materials. The difference between refractive indices in a given gem, called birefringence, is itself a useful measurement for identifying gemstones. Perhaps the best example of a strongly birefringent gem, where doubling of back facets is distinct, is zircon.

Dispersion and Brilliancy

White light is a mixture of wavelengths. In solid materials each wavelength travels at a different speed, and thus each has a distinct index of refraction. Isaac Newton first recorded this phenomenon in his experiments with glass prisms. Newton discovered that a prism can separate the component colors, or wavelengths, of white light by bending each a different amount. This is called dispersion.

Dispersion is important to the beauty of many gems, including zircon, diamond, sphene, and others. It is especially important in colorless stones that have no body color to make their appearance distinctive. The dispersion of a gem is the amount that individual light wavelengths are separated in the material. This effect can be enhanced by proper cutting. But basically the stronger the dispersion, the better the separation, and the more vivid the individual colors appear where different wavelengths emerge from the gem.

The brilliancy of a gem is the amount of light returned to the eye of the observer. Gems are faceted so that light entering them is reflected internally by the facets and flashed back to the viewer in a myriad of **23**

Calcite (opp. l.) is doubly refracting, causing a doubling of images. Dispersion (opp. r.) is the separation of white light into component colors, a feature well displayed by diamond.

sparkling rays. This effect can be achieved because light entering a gem is refracted, or bent. But the angles at which the facets are cut are very important. If the angles are wrongly matched to the gem's refractive power, light will not be returned to the viewer's eye. Instead it may pass directly through, or be reflected off to the side. The result is a gem that appears "dead" and lifeless. The term "fisheye" is sometimes used where the central portion of the stone lacks brilliancy. Factors that affect gem brilliancy include facet angles, transparency, the perfection of polish on facet surfaces, and the proportions of the gem. The proportions of a gem are the relative sizes of the crown, or upper portion, pavilion, or lower portion, and diameter measured at the girdle. The diameter of the table, or large top facet, is also important, as well as the overall height of the stone compared to the diameter.

Brilliancy and dispersion are most important in the case of diamonds. For centuries diamonds were cut primarily to maximize weight and size, and the scientific principles of cutting were not yet understood. Today many shops cut for maximum brilliancy and overall appearance. Many commercial diamonds suffer in attractiveness because of oversized tables, thin crowns, or overdeep pavilions. An expert can often tell which of these problems is present by the appearance of the stone to his eye. Since both maximum brilliancy and maximum dispersion cannot be achieved with the same set of angles and proportions, an "optimum" set of parameters has been worked out. Stones cut to these proportions and angles achieve high brilliancy and a great amount of dispersive "fire."

Specific Gravity

Specific gravity, sometimes called density, is the relative weight of a given volume of material compared to the weight of the same volume of water. Different substances have different degrees of compactness. A box full of light bulbs would have a lower density than an equal-sized box full of broken glass, because in the latter the glass is more compressed. Similar differences exist at an atomic scale, accounting for the differences in density of such materials as lead and aluminum.

Specific gravity, abbreviated S.G., is relatively constant in a given material. It is thus a useful identifying feature for gemstones. Special balances have been developed for measuring S.G. using the principles of buoyancy. This principle, discovered by Archimedes in ancient Greece, states basically that a floating object displaces an amount of water equal to its own volume that remains submerged. For example, a cut diamond and a cut aquamarine of identical size may displace equal volumes of water. But the diamond itself will weigh about 30 percent more than the aquamarine, because their respective specific gravities are 3.52 and 2.72. By comparison, an equal volume of lead, with S.G.

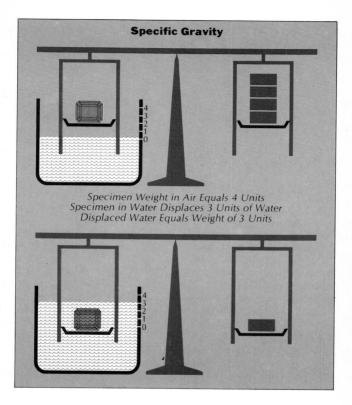

Specific Gravity

Specimen Weight in Air Equals 4 Units
Specimen in Water Displaces 3 Units of Water
Displaced Water Equals Weight of 3 Units

11.4, would weigh about three times as much as the diamond.

Specific gravity is useful in estimating the weight of gems. A one-carat round diamond would be smaller than a one-carat round aquamarine. Various synthetic gems have distinctive specific gravities. Some diamond imitations have S.G. values of 4.55 and 5.13, so different from diamond that identification of a loose stone may be a simple procedure. The easiest S.G. techniques involve special, heavy, organic liquids with known specific gravities. A gem will float in a liquid of higher S.G. and sink in a liquid of lower S.G. It will float at a fixed level in a matching S.G. liquid.

Luster and Fluorescence

Luster is the appearance of a material due to light reflected from its surface. The nature and irregularity of the surface affects the luster of **25** unpolished materials. Luster is a natural property that is characteristic of a material and is a function of its atomic structure. In the case of faceted gems, luster is affected by polishing. Polishing prevents the luster of a gem from being distinguishable in many cases, but luster can sometimes be a useful diagnostic tool.

Fluorescence is an optical effect arising from the movement of electrons within the structure of a material. The shifting of electrons may allow the material to "store" energy within its structure and release it at a later time. Input energy can be provided in various ways, but the most typical sources are ultraviolet ("blacklight"), x-rays, or an electric field.

Sometimes the absorption and release process is so rapid as to be instantaneous, and the phenomenon is called fluorescence. If the energy release is delayed for a period of minutes, hours, or days, it is called phosphorescence. These effects are useful when the released energy is in the form of visible light.

Fluorescence in gems is useful in identification, and is sometimes helpful in distinguishing natural from synthetic stones. The general technique is to irradiate a gem with ultraviolet light and observe the fluorescent color, if any. Some synthetic gems show strong fluorescence, whereas many natural stones contain impurities that "quench" fluorescence. Usually only those gems that fluoresce can display phosphorescence, which is an eerie afterglow that persists when the ultraviolet source light is removed. An advantage of fluorescence tests is that they are rapid, easy to perform, and non-destructive.

Gem Cutting

Gem cutting is one of the oldest arts. Crudely shaped beads and ornaments have been found in the ruins of some of the most ancient civilizations, and finely carved and polished objects were produced centuries before the birth of Christ.

A polish is nothing more than the absence of surface irregularities. Such irregularities diffuse and scatter reflected light, creating a dull aspect. As minor hills and valleys on the surface are worn off and the surface becomes smooth, light is more evenly reflected, giving a shine to the material and usually deepening its apparent color. A similar effect could be achieved by simply wetting the surface, because surface tension would cause the adhering water surface to be relatively smooth.

The most primitive form of lapidary, or gem cutting, was the fashioning of beads. Later the beads were ground into a more regular shape, such as a circle or an oval, and one side was ground flat. A cut gem with a rounded top and flat, convex or concave bottom is called a cabochon, from an Old French word meaning "head." By the 17th Century, sophisticated gem-cutting techniques were developed, culminating in **26** the art of faceting. This is the placement of regular, flat surfaces in a

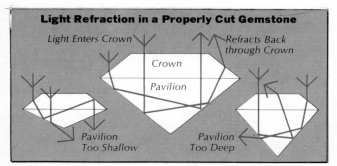

Light Refraction in a Properly Cut Gemstone

Light Enters Crown

Refracts Back through Crown

Crown

Pavilion

Pavilion Too Shallow

Pavilion Too Deep

pre-selected geometric pattern. Today, faceting is widely employed for cutting even inexpensive gems, and machines have been developed that can do much of the job automatically. But in many parts of the world, fine gem rough is still cut by hand, using relatively simple and unsophisticated tools, such as the so-called "jamb peg." In the hands of an expert, the jamb peg can produce results equal to any machine.

Gem cutting is a delicate business, especially with fragile stones and those that are difficult to polish. Each gem cutter develops his own style and his own special techniques. Cutting quality can make the difference between a magnificent gemstone with great brilliancy and a polished lump that displays little sparkle. A well-cut gem is generally more valuable than a poorly cut one, even when both gems were cut from rough of the same quality. In the case of diamond cutting plays a major

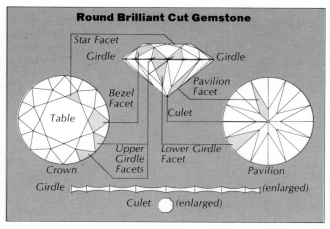

Round Brilliant Cut Gemstone

Star Facet

Girdle

Girdle

Bezel Facet

Pavilion Facet

Table

Culet

Upper Girdle Facets

Lower Girdle Facet

Crown

Pavilion

Girdle (enlarged)

Culet (enlarged)

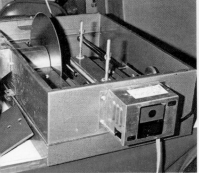

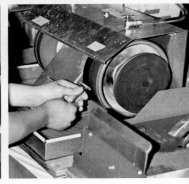

Faceting (r.) is a precision lapidary art. Initial steps in gem cutting are slabbing (below l.), followed by grinding and sanding (below r.)

role, because incorrect angles and proportions mean a drastic loss of brilliancy and fire, which are the chief attributes of diamond.

Cabochon cutting involves several distinctive steps. The rough material may be simply rounded off and polished to yield a free-form gem. Usually, however, the rough is first cut into slices called slabs. Slabbing is accomplished today by means of a diamond blade. This is simply a disc of metal the edge of which has been impregnated with diamond powder. The blade is not sharp, but as it is held against a rock, the diamond abrades the rock and allows the disc to penetrate. A cutting speed of 1 inch per minute is typical. After slices have been cut, a smaller saw, called a trim saw, is used to give rough outline to the desired cabochon. Next the gem is ground to shape with grinding wheels, usually made of aluminum oxide or silicon carbide. To make the stone easier to hold, it is generally cemented to a small dowel called a dop stick, using a special wax.

Grinding speed depends on the coarseness of the wheel. Each step removes scratches created by the previous step. After grinding, the normal procedure is sanding with successively finer grades of sandpaper. After fine sanding, a cabochon is usually shiny and smooth and may look almost polished. The final polish adds mirror-like brilliance and removes all traces of scratches.

Polishing a gem consists of progressively grinding the surface with finer and finer abrasives. Many kinds of abrasives have been used throughout history: crushed sand, garnet, corundum, emery, silicon carbide (a man-made material), and oxides of tin, cerium, and chromium are a few examples.

Typical cabochon shapes are circles, ovals, hearts, squares, teardrops, rectangles, and many special shapes. A buffed-top cabochon is one with a flat or gently rounded, rather than a high-domed, top.

Faceting involves the same sequence of grinding and polishing steps used to make cabochons. In faceting, the initial step is to cut a preform, a portion of gem material roughly the size and shape of the finished gem, but not yet containing facets. The preform is dopped, and the dop stick placed in a special device called a faceting head.

The faceting head is a modern convenience component that allows a stone to be precisely rotated and tilted to desired angles. Proper angles are desired to bring out the maximum brilliancy from a given gem. In many parts of the world faceting heads are not used. Instead, a special pole is employed, a vertical shaft less than a foot high in which are placed holes penetrating at various angles and positions. This pole, the jamb peg, provides the "angular settings" for cutting various gems. The cutter inserts the dop stick into one of these holes and rests the other end, to which the gem is attached, against a grinding wheel. Although the technique sounds primitive, in the hands of an expert it can produce remarkable results.

Each facet is ground on the preform, the cutter stopping the grinding process when his eye tells him that the facet has reached its correct size. Facets are ground by the action of abrasives against a flat, horizontally running disc called a lap. The process is called lapping. Each facet is individually ground, including the large facet on top called the table. A faceted gem is polished in the same way as a cabochon, with each facet undergoing successive fine-grinding stages and terminating with a polishing agent. Today various grit sizes of diamond are becoming increasingly popular among lapidaries. Diamond tremendously increases cutting speed, and produces a better polish.

Facets must be applied to both the top and bottom of a faceted gem. Since the gem must be held on a dop stick for cutting, only half the work can be completed at a time. When all the facets on one end are completely polished, the dop stick is placed in a special alignment jig. A second dop stick is attached to the polished end while the stone is still attached to the first stick. Then the original dop is carefully removed and the new dop stick inserted in the faceting head or jamb peg. The other end of the stone is completed in the same way as the first, making sure that the new facets are exactly lined up with the completed ones. **29**

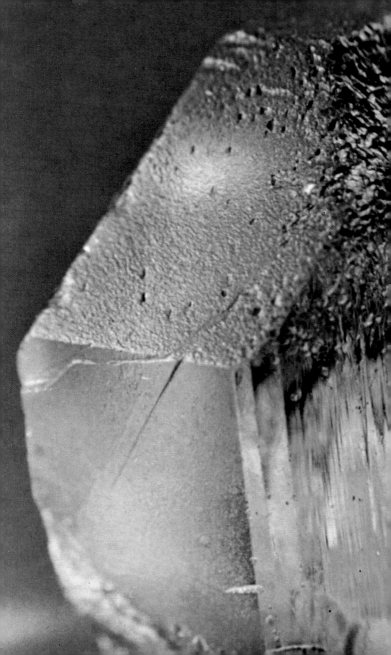

Gems and Gemstones

Most gems are cut from mineral crystals. Peridot, for example, is the gem form of olivine. This crystal is from St. John's Island in the Red Sea.

Diamond

Diamond is the best-known gem. Its history is so long and complex that the beginning is lost in antiquity.

India was a source of many of the world's most famous diamonds. Diamonds were traded in India as early as four centuries before the birth of Christ, many gems reaching Ceylon (now Sri Lanka) and the Middle East. Other stones found their way into the Roman Empire, where their supposed magical powers enhanced their value. Arabian and Persian merchants brought diamonds to China, where they served as jade-cutting and pearl-drilling tools in the first few centuries A.D. Diamond tools were highly regarded in China and were considered gifts worthy of royalty.

Indian superstitions about diamond eventually spread throughout the world. The Buddhists believed that a person's soul had to be purified before joining the "universal soul," or karma. The steps in this process involved incarnations as animals, plants, and even minerals. This fostered the belief that minerals and gems have life, a notion that persisted for centuries. The Greek philosopher Plato believed in life among gems and rated diamond as the noblest. Such ideas were held well into the Renaissance. Jerome Cardin who, in the 16th Century, first designated stones as "precious," believed that minerals and gems were "born" of the fluids in rock cavities.

Diamond, with its remarkable properties of hardness, dispersion, and brilliancy, was also considered a strong medicine. The powder of white, flawless diamonds would, if swallowed, impart health, energy, and long life. Flawed stones, however, might have the opposite effect! Diamond powder was for centuries considered to be a deadly poison, and the deaths of many prominent rulers and politicians were attributed to this agent. Diamond was supposed to have many other mystical powers. If held in the mouth, a diamond would cause the teeth to fall out. It repelled phantoms and demons, and prevented nightmares.

Diamond crystals (above) may be very symmetrical, but are not as spectacular as cut stones, such as this magnificent canary-yellow gem (opp.).

Diamonds could ward off magic and protect the wearer in battle by giving him courage, virtue, and invincibility.

Fabulous diamonds symbolized wealth and power. They were regarded as emblems of rank and status. In times of political upheaval and uncertainty, diamonds also represented easily portable wealth. The history of diamond constantly links together attributes of power, magic, and great value. The incredible beliefs about this gem have been embellished through the centuries. But they are undoubtedly derived from the truly remarkable properties that diamond does display.

Forms and Properties

Diamond is pure carbon, the element that is also the foundation of life. Carbon has interesting chemical properties that enable it to form a truly vast number of compounds with many other elements. Some of these are biologically active. Another form of pure carbon is the mineral graphite. Graphite is so easily powdered that it is used as the "lead" in pencils (mixed with clay for this application), and so greasy that it is widely used as a lubricant. Yet diamond is the hardest known substance, and will easily scratch any other material.

Forms and Colors

Diamond crystals occur in a variety of shapes and forms. The most common shape resembles two four-sided pyramids arranged base-to-base and is known as an octahedron, an eight-sided form. The directions of easy cleavage in diamond are parallel to the octahedral faces. Other forms seen on diamond crystals include the cube and dodecahedron, the latter an interesting 12-sided form. Some rough diamond crystals are combinations of several of these forms. Also frequently present on diamond crystal surfaces are triangular pits called trigons, believed to have formed during crystal growth.

Diamonds occur in a wide range of colors. The most familiar are basically white or colorless, usually with a tinge of yellow or gray. Richly colored stones, called fancies, are rare and highly prized. Fancy colors include golden-yellow, blue, green, pink, and amber.

Fine yellow diamonds with so-called "canary" color make notable gems. Two of the best-known yellow diamonds are the Florentine (137.5 carats) and the Tiffany (128.5 carats).

Brown and coffee-colored diamonds are not as rare, but are seldom seen in the trade. Orange diamonds are popular in South Africa, but few are sold in the United States. Green diamonds are very rare, the most famous being the Dresden green of 48.5 carats. Diamonds are occasionally found in a greenish-yellow hue, sometimes called "champagne color." Blue diamonds are extremely rare. By far the most famous is the Hope Diamond, weighing 44.5 carats, on display at the Smithsonian Institution in Washington, D.C. This remarkable gem has a somewhat metallic surface luster that reflects light and makes the gem appear darker than it actually is. Pale-blue diamonds are also known, and violet gems are occasionally found. Pale-red and pink diamonds are very rare and although red diamonds have been reported, an intense, fine, red gem has not yet been authenticated. Brownish-red diamonds, on the other hand, are occasionally seen in the diamond trade.

Localities and Formation

Diamonds are found in various parts of the world. In past centuries fine diamonds came from India. This is the world's oldest major source of diamonds, and supplied stones for centuries to all parts of the globe. Indian diamonds are found in riverbeds. These stones were weathered out of source rocks and concentrated in streams over a period of many years. Such river deposits are termed alluvial, and Indian alluvial deposits were worked as early as 800 B.C. Much of our information about old Indian workings comes from the writings of the great traveler Tavernier, who lived and traveled in the 17th Century. Most of the Indian diamonds came from an area known as Golconda. Other Indian deposits include those of the Brahamani River, the Panna diamond fields,

and the mines of Sumelpur.

In the early part of the 18th Century, diamonds were discovered in Brazil, in an area later called Diamantina. They were not easy to sell because it was feared that a flood of Brazilian stones would depress diamond prices. To avoid the stigma placed on Brazilian diamonds, dealers sent them to India, where they were marketed as Indian gems. Later diamonds were also found in Bahia and near Bagagem, Brazil. Brazilian diamonds, like the Indian gems, are found as alluvium in riverbeds and stream deposits.

Diamonds are found in Venezuela (all alluvial), Guyana, Borneo, and Australia. A diamond mine at Murfreesboro, Arkansas has yielded many small stones, as well as a few larger ones. The Uncle Sam Diamond, weighing 40.23 carats in the rough, was the largest diamond ever discovered in North America. It yielded a 12.42 carat emerald cut gem now in a private collection. The Murfreesboro deposit has been worked for years by visitors who would pay a small fee for the privilege **35**

A faceted diamond is brilliant, because it returns considerable light to the eye of the viewer, and also dispersive, because the light is split up into rainbow colors.

of indulging in "diamond-hunting fever." Small diamonds are still occasionally found.

Some diamonds have been found in Canada, in glacial deposits. These deposits were accumulated by glacial action that scoured vast portions of the country, and the source rocks have never been discovered. The U.S.S.R. is currently a leading producer of diamonds, in fact the world's largest outside Africa. Mining conditions are very difficult due to the extreme cold.

The vast majority of the world's gem diamond comes from Africa. The first diamond discovered in Africa was found by a child in 1867. Within a few years a "diamond rush" had started in South Africa that helped to develop this rich and beautiful country.

Diamond Mining

The history of diamond mining in Africa is colorful and filled with intrigue. Fortunes were made overnight in South Africa between 1870 and 1910, and such famous names as Cecil Rhodes and Ernest Oppenheimer stand out as dominant in this period. Some of the most famous mines are the Dutoitspan, Kimberley, Wesselton, De Beers, Bultfontein, and Jagersfontein. The largest diamond ever found was discovered at the Premier Mine in South Africa. Named the Cullinan Diamond after the mine owner, it weighed 3,106 carats, or about 1½ pounds, in the rough. This is a staggering size, but nonetheless it has been speculated that the diamond found was only ⅓ of a much larger parent stone that apparently broke up within the host rock. The other pieces were never found. The Cullinan was cut into 105 stones, the largest two of which remain the largest cut diamonds in the world: the Cullinan I weighing 530.2 carats, and the Cullinan II of 317.4 carats. Both gems are in the British Crown Jewels in the Tower of London.

Diamonds are found in Zaire in a huge area of alluvial deposits.

Most are industrial grade, but the production is enormous. Ghana produces quantities of small stones of poor quality. Sierra Leone produces fine gem diamonds, some of large size, mostly from alluvial deposits. In 1972 the world's third-largest rough diamond was discovered in Sierra Leone. Named the Star of Sierra Leone, the massive 968.9-carat rough was cut into 11 fine white gems, the largest of which weighs 143.2 carats.

Other African diamonds come from South West Africa, Tanzania, Guinea, the Ivory Coast, Gabon, Cameroun, Rhodesia, Liberia, the Republic of the Congo, and Nyasaland (Malawi). Annual world diamond production is approximately 50 million carats. Africa produces most of the gem diamonds found, with the U.S.S.R. holding second place. Only about a quarter of all diamonds mined are of gem quality.

Mining Methods and Marketing

Diamonds occur in an igneous rock called kimberlite, which formed under conditions of great heat and pressure. In mining, kimberlite is extracted by either open pit or underground mining operations. The rock is then crushed to a fine-particle size. Diamonds have a higher specific gravity than the enclosing rock, so they tend to be concentrated in various washing and settling operations. A final concentrate is then washed across a grease table, to which the diamonds stick while waste materials wash off. The grease is periodically scraped off and melted to recover the diamonds.

In a typical diamond deposit there is about one carat of diamond in every five tons of rock. Of this, only about 20 percent is gem quality, and half the rough material is lost in cutting. Therefore, to produce a half-carat cut diamond might require the mining of as much as 50 tons of rock.

The history of diamond mining glitters with tales of adventure, vast wealth, and powerful men. Over a period of years, control of the South African diamond mines eventually came under the influence of a single large company, De Beers Consolidated Mines, Ltd., a publicly held stock company. Through its subsidiaries and contracts with other companies, De Beers controls the mining and marketing of more than ¾ of the world's diamonds. This centralization of control results in great price stability, which has proven beneficial to the jewelry trade.

After mining and initial sorting, diamonds are sold to the Diamond Trading Company, owned by De Beers, which sorts them into smaller parcels. These parcels are sold to invited buyers at special sales called "sights." The parcels are selected by the Trading Company, and the buyers have only the choice of buying or not buying what they are offered. If many buyers do not accept their parcels, the Trading Com-

Diamonds occur in a volcanic rock called kimberlite (opp.). Such matrix specimens are extremely rare and desired by collectors of minerals.

pany may stockpile diamonds through its selling agent, the Central Selling Corporation.

The diamonds purchased at sights are then sold to cutters. At every stage in the diamond-selling process, careful attention is paid to correct valuation. The sight buyer must know in detail the needs of the cutters who are his customers, and the cutters must closely estimate the size and value of diamonds that can be cut from their rough.

Diamond Cutting

Diamonds could not be cut at all if not for the fact that the hardness of diamond is not uniform. The point of an octahedron, for example, is harder than the surface of an octahedral face. Thus, powdered diamond can cut into a diamond crystal and abrade its surface because the powder will always contain some particles oriented in a ''hard'' direction.

Early diamond jewels were primarily talismans, so the stones did not have to be polished and rough crystals were used. The art of diamond cutting originated in Venice in the early part of the 14th Century and spread to Paris and Antwerp. Today, London is the trade center for rough diamonds. From here they are sent to Antwerp, Bombay, Tel Aviv, Johannesburg, New York, San Juan, Amsterdam, and other cities for cutting. Russian-made diamonds are also appearing on the market in steadily growing numbers.

There are several steps in diamond cutting. The first gives initial shape to the stone, and is known as cleaving. Diamond readily splits in directions parallel to the octahedral faces, and cleaving rapidly removes unwanted material or separates rough into portions which are separately fashioned.

An alternative to cleaving is sawing, a step that is also useful in removing flawed areas from a diamond. A modern diamond saw is a small disc of phosphor-bronze whose edge is impregnated with diamond powder. In times past, sawing was done with a length of fine wire, a tremendously laborious and time-consuming job. It is reported that it took almost a year to saw the 410-carat Regent Diamond in half. Today the operation would require only a few days.

The next step, called bruting, consists of rounding the corners of the octahedron. This was originally done by hand with a diamond tool called a sharp, and is done today by machine. The modern equivalent of bruting is called rounding up. Small flaws can also be removed in the rounding-up process, and weight loss kept to a minimum. Occasionally a small portion of the original diamond crystal surface is left on the girdle of the stone. This area, called a natural, indicates that little material was wasted in cutting, although its presence is not desirable on a finished diamond.

Prior to cutting,
a diamond is marked (l.)
to indicate cleavage
planes, and then cleaved
(center, Lazare Kaplan
International).
The bruting or girdling
operation (btm.)
gives rough shape
to the cut stone.

After rounding up, the diamond is faceted. The table facet and the first 16 facets (eight on top, eight on the bottom) are put on by the blocker or lapper. Diamond faceting is a precision art, and the cutting wheel, which is a cast-iron lap, must be carefully balanced and running true. The diamond cutter relies on his eye to correctly proportion and finish the stone.

Next, the brillianteerer places the final 40 facets, and polishes them. Brillianteering requires more skill than blocking, and an experienced craftsman can often correct small errors made in blocking. The final step in diamond cutting is a careful check of the work, and a thorough cleaning by boiling in acid to remove all traces of oil, dirt, and diamond powder.

The most popular diamond cut is the round brilliant, a cut often credited to a (perhaps mythical) 16th-Century Venetian lapidary named Vincenzio Perruzzi. The natural shape of the octahedron lends itself to a rounded form with a pointed bottom and flat top, but various proportions and angles could be used. Only in the 20th Century has modern mathematical theory, combined with centuries of trial-and-error experience, revealed a set of ideal proportions and angles for extracting the maximum brilliance and dispersive color from a diamond.

Evaluating Gem Diamonds

The value of a gem diamond depends on several factors: size, color, clarity, cutting quality, and correct proportions.

40   Large diamonds are rarer than small ones, and therefore more

The final step in diamond cutting is polishing, accomplished with rapidly spinning wheels and diamond powder abrasives (Lazare Kaplan International).

valuable. The price of a diamond does not go up in simple steps along with size, however. A three-carat gem will cost far more, per carat, than three times that of a one-carat stone of comparable quality. In the past few years the number of larger crystals being mined in Africa has been slowly decreasing; and the typical gem crystal found is becoming smaller and smaller. This creates a much higher premium on larger stones. Fashion does have some effect on prices. Dealers find that in some years gems between ½ and one carat are in greatest demand and large stones do not sell quickly. In other years the reverse may be true.

Color is the most important single factor that contributes to the value of a gem diamond. Several grading scales are currently in use; on the GIA scale, for example, the highest-quality color grades are D, E, and F, all corresponding to a pure "white" color, with no tinge of yellow. Further along in the scale, corresponding to moving through the alphabet to N, O, and P, a diamond would have an increasingly yellowish tint, and its value would drop steadily, all other factors being constant. If the yellow became very strong and attractive the diamond might, however, be considered a "fancy color," and its value would be much higher than that of a so-called "off-color" stone.

To the untrained eye, two gems may both appear "white," whereas one might actually be F and the other J on the GIA scale, and the difference in price could be as much as 35 percent. Color grading can only be done accurately by comparing a stone with a "master set" of graded gems of the same general size. The diamonds should be examined through the back, on a white background, and with a standard illumination. Obviously grading is not a simple matter, and should always be done by someone trained in the techniques. The lighting is especially critical, and the best illumination for diamond grading is a filtered, cool-white, fluorescent lamp.

Clarity refers to the presence of inclusions, spots, or flaws in a gem. Most gemstones contain inclusions of other minerals, which were incorporated at the time of crystal growth. Inclusions decrease the value of a diamond. Their size and number can be determined by means of a magnifying glass or microscope.

In the past the term "perfect" has been widely used in the gem trade to indicate a flawless diamond. The term "perfect" is a poor one and should be completely abandoned. The Federal Trade Commission regards as "flawless" a diamond that contains no "flaws, cracks, carbon spots, clouds, or other blemishes or imperfections of any sort" when examined at a magnification of 10X by a trained eye.

A useful system of clarity grading has been devised by the Gemological Institute of America. It assesses diamonds according to the size, location, and number of inclusions and blemishes present. Gems containing no such imperfections are considered flawless (F). With increasing size and number of imperfections, the classifications are very very slightly imperfect (VVSI), very slightly imperfect (VSI), slightly imperfect (SI) and imperfect (I). Each of these categories has two subdivisions, labeled 1 and 2 as subscripts. Some inclusions may be so small that they are not readily visible to the naked eye, and don't materially affect the appearance of a cut gem. However, their presence does materially affect the diamond's value. Truly flawless diamonds are exceedingly scarce and very expensive. Sometimes imperfections near the girdle of a diamond are hidden by the setting. In addition, the true color of a set diamond cannot be determined. For these reasons, diamond grading can only be accomplished with unset stones.

The surface finish and polish of a diamond, as well as its proportions, affect its beauty and hence its value. As mentioned earlier, maximum brilliance and maximum dispersion cannot be achieved in a single stone with one set of angles and proportions. The ideal case would be a compromise, involving proportions and angles that would give brilliance and also substantial dispersive color. Some diamonds are cut to these dimensions, and such gems are indeed spectacular and beautiful. But most of the diamonds sold commercially do not have "ideal" proportions. This is because acceptable appearance can be achieved with less stringent requirements, but at the same time the cutter can produce larger stones from his rough material.

Diamond, long a symbol of wealth and power, has been synthesized in the laboratory. To date, only a few crystals of a size suitable for gem

Diamonds must be sorted according to size and color for grading (above). A collection of colored diamonds is one of the rarest groups of natural objects known (opp.).

use (up to one carat) have been grown. These were so expensive to manufacture, however, that at the present time they cannot compete with natural diamonds in the gem market.

Diamond is one of the loveliest of all gems. Its hardness is superior to that of any other stone, and its optical properties are unique among natural gems. Good marketing has created for the diamond an aura of extravagance and glamour. Yet tight international control of the diamond-marketing structure has meant price stability and solidity that benefits the entire jewelry industry.

Consumer Tips—The purchase of a diamond can be a major investment, or mark an event of great personal significance, such as a marriage or engagement. Pitfalls include misuse by the seller of certain misleading terms, such as "perfect," or "blue-white." The FTC has established trade practice rules for the jewelry industry that prohibit the use of such terms except in rigorous circumstances. Rapid sight estimates of quality are untrustworthy, even from an expert. A stone should be graded under proper circumstances, with the right equipment, and this can best be done with unset gems. Wholesale and retail prices of diamonds vary enormously, but the wholesale value of a correctly graded and described diamond can be fairly accurately determined. A typical description of a diamond might read as follows: "Size 1.24 carats, color J, SI_2, no deduction for proportions or finish." The color is not white, and the clarity grade SI_2 indicates the presence of several inclusions and blemishes. These factors would mean that the value of the diamond is not as great as that of a flawless, white, perfectly proportioned gem weighing 1.24 carats, by comparison. The stone in question might be worth only 35 percent as much. The exact percentage is determined by the exact color and clarity grade.

Beryl

Color varieties of beryl include: emerald (green), aquamarine (blue, blue-green), morganite (pink, pale yellow-orange), goshenite (colorless), and heliodor, or golden beryl (yellow, orange).

Beryl crystals occur throughout the world. Non-gemmy crystals can reach dimensions of several feet and weigh many tons. The mineral, consisting of beryllium aluminum silicate, is the chief ore of beryllium and is mined extensively for this metal content. Gem beryl, of course, is usually not ground up as ore. Emerald crystals never reach very large size, but huge, transparent masses of aquamarine and other color varieties have been found. Occasionally giant-sized gems are cut from such crystals, but these thousand-carat baubles are museum curiosities rather than jewelry items.

Pure beryl is completely colorless. Traces of impurities present during crystal growth cause the color variations. The blue of aquamarine and the yellow of heliodor are both due to the presence of iron. Chromium produces the rich green color of emerald. Some green beryls colored by iron are occasionally marketed as emerald, but technically they should not be so termed.

The occurrence of emerald is basically different from that of other beryls. Emerald is found in metamorphic rocks, where the mode of formation restricts crystal size. Other beryls are typically found in pegmatites, which normally produce crystals of large size.

Emerald was dedicated by the Greeks to the goddess Venus. Cleopatra's emerald mines in Egypt were worked as early as 2000 B.C. and provided many stones for the craftsmen of the ancient world. For centuries emerald has been a wellspring of mystery and superstition. It is the symbol of immortality and of faith. It was once believed that gazing at an emerald was beneficial to the eyes. The subtle change of color that the gem sometimes displays was thought to verify the inconsistency of lovers. The magical powers of emerald are no longer believed, yet the gem still does possess a definite mystique. It is one of the most highly prized of all gems, as well as one of the rarest and most valuable.

Emeralds weighing more than several carats are extremely rare and costly. A fine stone of good color, which is a deep green with no tinge of yellow or blue, and free of inclusions and flaws, may cost several thousand dollars per carat. Large gems of this type may sell for as much as $20,000 per carat.

The best-known locality for emerald is Colombia, where the mines have produced steadily for centuries. In the U.S.S.R. emeralds have been produced since about 1830, when a peasant noted some green stones at the foot of a tree uprooted by a storm. Russian emeralds are

Colors of beryl include the green of emerald and the golden yellow of heliodor (top). Cut gems of aquamarine, green beryl, and golden beryl from Brazil are popular (btm.).

deep green, but not of the best hue, and crystals have yielded only small stones that are relatively free of inclusions and flaws. Brazilian emeralds have been avidly sought since the middle of the 16th Century. The lure of "green wealth" helped to open up the interior of this vast country. Some of this emerald is of fine quality, almost on a par with Colombian material. Though much exploration has been done, no deposits of emerald comparable to those of Colombia have been found elsewhere in South America.

The Colombian emerald mines at Muzo and Chivor have produced the finest emeralds known. Pizarro, after his conquest of Peru, sent back to Spain numerous emeralds of fantastic size and quality. It is said that the ancient Peruvians worshipped, among other things, a fine emerald the size of an ostrich egg. Today the Colombian government operates the emerald mines. Since 1934 all persons involved in the cutting and selling of Colombian emeralds have had to register with the government, and exports are strictly controlled.

Emeralds are known from Australia, South Africa, Rhodesia, Zam-
46 bia, Tanzania, Norway, and India, but these are far less important than

Golden beryl (above) makes a spectacular gem when well cut. Aquamarine (opp.) sometimes forms large crystals, but rarely of top gem quality.

the Colombian deposits. Fine emeralds have been recovered in North Carolina, and excellent quality stones in the 10–20 carat range have been cut from such material.

Emeralds have characteristic inclusions by which they can be identified and distinguished from the many synthetic, or man-made, emeralds produced in recent years.

Aquamarine is, next to emerald, the most highly prized of the beryls. The color of aquamarine may vary from pale blue to a rich and deep blue or blue-green. A lovely blue color may also be produced by heating some greenish-yellow beryl. In ancient times beryls "the color of the sea" were considered the most desirable, but today's fashion demands the deeper blue stones. These are in great demand and the price of fine aquamarine has risen steadily in recent years. Retail prices of several hundred dollars per carat are not uncommon.

Very subtle differences in shade and depth of color accompany radical differences in cost. Extensive familiarity with beryls and experience in handling aquamarine is needed to accurately appraise gems and gem rough. In general, the deeper the color of a beryl, the greater its value.

The principal localities for aquamarine are Brazil (notably the region known as Minas Gerais), South West Africa, India, the Malagasay Republic, and the U.S.S.R. There are many United States localities for blue beryl, but few are of gem significance.

Cat's-eye beryl (r.) is a curiosity seldom available commercially. Morganite (below) is a lovely gem, and stones larger than this 47.2-carat one are available.

Morganite, heliodor (golden beryl), and **goshenite** are not widely known to the gem-buying public. Most gem material comes from Brazil, although fine rough has been found in the Malagasay Republic, South West Africa, and San Diego County, California. Gem morganite of superb quality has been mined in Pala, California, along with some of the finest tourmaline crystals known. Morganite was named after the New York banker and gem collector, J. P. Morgan. The name heliodor means "gift of the sun," which is appropriate for the yellow color. Pale-green beryl, not colored by chromium, is simply termed "green beryl." An unusual red beryl is found in Utah, but has no gem significance.

The most popular cutting style for emerald and most of the other
48 beryls is a step-cut rectangle with the corners truncated, yielding a

characteristic shape known as the *emerald cut*. Other popular beryl cuts include the cushion cut, a simple rectangle; the octagon, which is basically a square emerald cut; and the round brilliant.

The beryls are all fairly tough gems, with the exception of emerald. Because of its typically present inclusions and flaws, emerald is a fragile gem and requires care in mounting and wear. The hardness of beryl is 7½–8 on the Mohs scale, which is ample for ringstones.

Occasionally a beryl contains fibrous inclusions, and a cabochon cut from such material will yield a weak cat's-eye. Stones that resemble emerald, such as peridot, tourmaline, green zircon, and demantoid, can be easily distinguished on the basis of optical properties. But to the naked eye even a glass imitation can sometimes be deceptive.

Consumer Tips—Many emeralds on the market have been treated with oil, typically grape-seed oil. This oil, which may even sometimes be colored green, seeps into fractures in the gems and makes them far less obvious. The oil can usually be detected with ultraviolet light.

Synthetic emeralds are often manufactured *with* inclusions, to appear more realistic. These inclusions are characteristic of the manufacturing process and can usually be identified by a trained gemologist.

Many synthetic emeralds are currently available, manufactured with various techniques. The prices are substantially lower than those of emeralds of comparable quality, and most synthetics manufactured are of extremely fine color. Some of these are virtually flawless, a condition seldom found in natural emerald. Synthetics may be marketed as "created emerald," "simulated emerald," or just "synthetic emerald."

Major price factors for emerald are: hue and depth of color, especially the presence or absence of a tinge of yellow (the latter is more desirable); freedom from inclusions and flaws; size; quality of cutting. Large, flawless emeralds are among the scarcest of all gems.

Aquamarines are frequently free of flaws, and the major price consideration is hue and intensity of color; in fine aquamarines absence of inclusions and flaws is taken for granted. Pale-colored stones are quite inexpensive, whereas the price of an aquamarine may soar as the color deepens, especially if there is no tinge of green. Large stones, weighing tens of carats, are available. Synthetic aquamarines are not commercially manufactured, but several blue gems that strongly resemble aquamarines are available. These include blue topaz and various synthetic imitations, such as blue spinel and glass.

An attractive blue aquamarine may originally have been a yellowish beryl that was heat-treated. The color change is permanent, however, and there is no way to prove that the color of a gem is or is not natural. Other artificially produced colors may present a problem, however, as fully discussed on pages 148–149. **49**

Corundum

Few gems have the mysterious depth of color, the glittering history, and the aristocratic dignity of the corundum gems. Pure corundum is colorless. The red variety is termed ruby. Blue corundum is called sapphire. All other colors are simply termed sapphire with a color-designating prefix, such as green sapphire, pink sapphire, and so on.

Corundum is aluminum oxide. It occurs throughout the world in various kinds of rocks, sometimes in large crystals. But crystals of rich color that have transparent areas large enough to yield gems are very scarce, and fine rubies and sapphires are therefore highly prized and very costly.

To the Hindus ruby, the Lord of Gems, seemed to burn with a kind of inextinguishable fire, capable of boiling water. According to the Greeks, it could melt wax on which it was impressed. The ruby was believed to exert powerful forces. It could guard a home or orchards against storms. It could preserve mental and bodily health. It could control passion and amorous thoughts, reconcile disputes, warm the corpses of mummies, and, if taken internally, even cure hemorrhages and other illnesses. The Burmese believed that if a ruby was embedded in the flesh of its owner by inflicting an intentional wound, its presence would confer invulnerability.

Sapphires were believed to attract divine favor to their owners. A gem could preserve its wearer from envy, protect against captivity, and serve as a key to understanding the sayings of oracles. Sapphire is the gem of autumn, and of the soul. The Bishop of Rennes in the 12th Century praised the virtues of the sapphire and started the long history of the use of this gem in church regalia.

A gem can be called ruby only if it is a corundum of a red or purple-red hue and medium to dark in shade. A pink or light-red corundum would more properly be called a pink sapphire. The finest rubies known come from Burma, although Burma also produces stones of lesser quality. The finest red-colored Burmese gems have been called "pigeon's-blood," and the most important producing area in Burma centers around the city of Mogok. Rubies have been mined here for more than 700 years. The geology is distinguished by the presence of very old metamorphic rocks and large bodies of marble, both of which are cut by pegmatite dikes. This has given rise to a huge variety of minerals, and no other locality in the world produces as great a wealth of gem minerals. Most rubies on the market today come from other localities, however, and are not as fine as Burmese gems.

The gem minerals were eroded from their parent rocks in ancient geologic time periods, and then concentrated by streams in beds of

Ruby crystals
from Burma (above)
are rare and valuable.
Cut Burmese rubies, set
with diamonds (l.),
provide truly elegant
and valuable jewelry.

51

gravel. Over the centuries the gravel beds became buried by soil to a depth of as much as 15 feet. Mining of the gem gravels involves removal of this overburden, or tunneling into it from a vertical shaft dug by hand. All the gems are mined by primitive hand methods, involving wire baskets in which the gravels are washed and sifted, and several stages of sorting.

Sri Lanka (Ceylon) also produces ruby and sapphire, especially in the area around Ratnapura, which in Singhalese means "city of gems."

Sapphires (top) occur in almost every color, and are brilliant when properly cut. The most popular sapphire color is a deep blue, which is often improved by setting with diamonds (btm.).

Mining methods here are similar to those in Burma, and the occurrence of gemstones is also in lenses or pockets of gravel buried at some depth. Ceylon ruby tends to be paler than material from Burma, but Ceylon sapphires are among the world's finest. Ceylonese sapphires in shades of pale blue, violet, deep blue, yellow, white, green, greenish-blue, brown, and pink are known, as well as a distinctive pinkish-orange shade known as "padparadsha."

Rubies from Thailand (Siam) tend to be dark purple-red or brownish-red, resembling garnets, although some pink stones are also found. Thai sapphires, especially greenish-yellow and grayish-blue stones, are of fair quality; the most notable locality is the Chantabun area, and a place called Battambang, which is now within the borders of Cambodia. Cambodia today is an important source of fine sapphires, especially the locality known as Pailin. Many fine black star sapphires come from Cambodia also.

Some of the world's most famous sapphires come from India, in the Vale of Kashmir high in the Himalayas. The fine blue gems found here have been known for about 100 years, but because of the high elevation mining can be carried out only a few months of the year. India also produces ruby and star ruby, though of poor quality. The Indian sources are very ancient, and some were known at the time of Marco Polo.

Australia is known for its production of very dark blue and blue-green sapphires, especially from Anakie, Queensland. Corundum gems of other colors have also been mined here. Gem corundum occurs in the United States in North Carolina and Montana. The mines at Macon County, North Carolina are open to the public on a fee basis, but no really fine gems occur here. Near Helena, Montana, sapphires occur in alluvial deposits and were recovered in gold-mining operations. The best known corundum deposit in North America is at Yogo Gulch in Fergus County, Montana. Here sapphires are found that yield fine blue gems up to 3–4 carats in weight, but most of the stones found are smaller. The crystals from Yogo Gulch tend to be flattened and plate-like, whereas corundum usually occurs in barrel-shaped crystals.

Corundum crystallizes in six-sided forms, as dictated by the internal atomic arrangement of the mineral. When corundum crystals form, they occasionally incorporate inclusions of other minerals, one of which is rutile (titanium oxide). Rutile tends to occur in elongated or fibrous crystals; such crystals within corundum orient themselves according to the six-fold symmetry of the corundum host material. Light is reflected from the rutile needles, producing a diffuse "sheen." When a cabochon is cut from such material, the reflections are sharpened along the curved upper surface of the stone. This is the phenomenon of asterism, and the six-fold symmetry of corundum produces a six-rayed star.

Star rubies and sapphires are rare gems, but they can be large and spectacular. The finest star ruby known weighs 138 carats; this is the famous Rosser Reeves star ruby, on display at the Smithsonian Institution in Washington, D.C. The world's largest blue star sapphire, the Star of India, exhibited at the American Museum of Natural History in New York, weighs 563 carats. Star corundum of lesser size is available in the gem trade in a wide variety of colors and degrees of transparency. Star gems are never completely transparent, because the star can only be produced by the presence of needle-like inclusions that cause some degree of turbidity. Each set of oriented inclusions produces one ray of the star. Only a properly cut gem, however, will display a perfectly centered, six-rayed star. This must be cut so that the base of the stone is perpendicular to the direction of six-fold symmetry of the corundum crystal.

In hardness corundum is second only to diamond, and rates 9 on the Mohs scale. Cut gems are both hard and tough, and wear extremely well in all kinds of jewelry.

Ruby and emerald are the most valuable of all gems. A large, essentially flawless, deep-red ruby weighing more than ten to 15 carats might cost more than $30,000 per carat. Small gems of lesser color might cost as little as $100 per carat. Sapphires are much less expensive, ranging in price from a few dollars per carat to several thousand dollars per carat. Colors other than blue are not very expensive; attractive star gems in shades of gray or black might sell for $10 to $50 per carat.

The red color of ruby is due to a trace of chromium. The blue of sapphire is due to the presence of iron and titanium; other colors are produced by various impurities. Although the term "sapphire" refers to gems of various colors, the name comes from the word "sapphirus," meaning "blue."

As with all gems, the value of corundum gems depends on color, clarity, and the quality of cutting. Poorly cut gems are "dead" and lifeless, whereas good proportions yield tremendous sparkle and brilliance in a sapphire or ruby. Corundum crystals are often color-zoned, and streakiness in a cut gem reduces its value. The most highly esteemed sapphire color is a medium blue with a slight tinge of violet. Colors other than blue are generally regarded as collector items, except for yellow and green gems that are available in fair quantity.

In the case of star corundum the color, centering of the star, the sharpness of the star, and the proportion of the weight concentrated above the girdle are important factors in valuation. The star should have no missing rays and should be clearly visible under a single light source. Greater transparency usually indicates greater value, and in all cases
larger stones are more valuable than smaller ones.

larger stones are more valuable than smaller ones.

Consumer Tips—Corundum has been synthesized in the laboratory since the latter part of the 19th Century, and today millions of carats are manufactured annually. This will be discussed in a later chapter. The gem buyer should, however, be aware that extremely fine corundum gems on sale at seemingly "bargain prices" are likely to be synthetics and actually worth a few pennies per carat. Rubies in antique jewelry do not have to be genuine just because they are old!

The high price of rubies and fine sapphires warrants caution in buying. At least five different methods are used to manufacture ruby, and it may require a well-equipped gemological lab and experienced gemologists to authenticate a stone. Star corundums are also made by various manufacturers, and some look deceptively like natural gems.

Rubies and sapphires make fine ringstones. They are brilliant gems and when properly cut catch and return considerable light to the viewer. Faceted corundum gems weighing more than ½ carat may be expensive. However, the small stones generally used in cluster rings that weigh only five or ten points are not expensive. This is an important buying consideration, because a ring, for example, with ½ carat of small blue sapphires may be worth far less than a comparable ring with a single ½ carat stone.

Many star corundums are cut with convex bottoms, rather than flat bottoms as with most cabochons. In some cases a higher percentage of the weight of a star sapphire may be located below the girdle than above it. The customer is therefore paying for material that will be completely hidden by the setting. The best value in a star corundum will therefore have a relatively flat bottom and have most of the weight of the stone visible and polished. All six legs of the star should be straight; the star should be well centered and clearly visible under a single light source. **55**

Star sapphires exist in a wide
variety of colors, but the most popular
is a medium shade of blue.

Garnet

Garnet is not a single mineral, but rather a group of similar minerals known as the "garnet group." All the natural garnets are complex silicates that differ in chemical composition, but have almost identical atomic structures. Garnets are not only red; they may be orange, yellow, brown, pale green, deep green, violet, purple, or even colorless.

Garnet is a truly ancient gem, known thousands of years before the birth of Christ. In those early days of civilization garnet, along with other gems, was known as "carbuncle." Although this term was generally applied to any red gem, today only red cabochon-cut garnets are called carbuncles. As with most other stones, garnets were considered to have great curative powers, especially against fevers. The wearer of a garnet was supposed to be protected in his travels and kept in good health. The name "garnet" comes from the Latin word "granatus," meaning "like seeds," because garnets in a rock look somewhat like the seeds in a pomegranate.

The Victorian era made extensive use of reddish garnets mined in Bohemia (now Czechoslovakia). These became quite popular and were widely used in low-cost jewelry, thus popularizing garnet as a gem and,

untortunately, cheapening its image. Reddish-brown garnets are still very inexpensive, although red, violet, and purple gems can be fairly costly, especially in larger sizes.

Garnet, with its large range of colors, is perhaps the most underrated of all gems. Nearly all the garnet species have gem potential. They are all about the same hardness, 6½–7½ on the Mohs scale, and none show cleavage, thus making them suitable for any type of jewelry. Cut garnets can be very brilliant and show rich, lovely colors that look good both in sunlight and in artificial light.

There are basically six major garnet species:

Pyrope is usually blood-red in color, sometimes with a tinge of purple or brown. Finer grades may resemble ruby. Most pyropes have some inclusions, and fine gem material is scarce, especially rough that will provide large cut gems. Such material is known from only a few localities. The U.S.S.R. is a source of magnificent gemstones. Good pyrope is associated with the diamond in South African kimberlite pipes. Brazil and Australia have produced good stones, and pyrope has been found in the United States in Arizona, Colorado, and New Mexico.

Almandine today satisfies world demand for an inexpensive red gemstone. Almandine is the most common garnet seen in jewelry. Its color

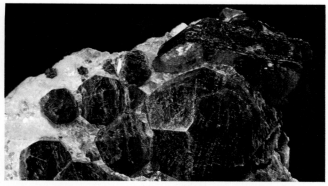

Grossular crystals from Asbestos, Quebec (opp.) are prized by mineral collectors, as are the fine crystals from North Carolina (top). Green, vanadium-rich garnets from Kenya (btm.) are rare gemstones.

ranges from dark red to brownish-red. The finer grades are almost indistinguishable at sight from pyrope. Good gem material comes from Sri Lanka, India, Brazil, Alaska, and Africa.

It is virtually impossible to visually determine if a garnet is a pyrope or an almandine. The distinguishing characteristics are in chemical composition and certain physical properties. Therefore a red garnet labeled almandine might actually be pyrope, or vice versa. In most cases the difference in value is not sufficient to warrant extensive analysis.

Spessartine is an uncommon garnet, usually reddish-brown to yellow-orange in color. Large stones may be deep orangy-red. Gem quality material is normally scarce, but sporadic discoveries may temporarily provide the market with ample gems to satisfy existing demand. The most prominent localities are Brazil, the Malagasay Republic (Madagascar), Sri Lanka, Burma, and the Rutherford Mine at Amelia Court House, Virginia. The gem mines of San Diego County, California have also produced fine spessartine, and a few small crystals were once dug up in building excavations on 179th Street in Manhattan.

Grossular, the most colorful of the garnets, is little known in the gem trade. Its delicate color varieties make exceptional gems. The dispersion of grossular garnet is higher than most other gems, and properly cut gems have tremendous brilliance and color. The other garnet species also have considerable dispersion, but their body color is usually so dark that the dispersion colors are masked. Typical grossular colors are colorless, pale green, yellowish-green, and cinnamon-brown, as well as orange, yellow, and a deep green resembling the color of fine emerald. This latter garnet, discovered in recent years in Tanzania and Kenya, is colored by vanadium. Grossular, however, is less fragile than emerald, and is also more brilliant. Vanadium grossular is extremely scarce, and stones weighing more than five carats may sell for more than $1,000 per carat.

Localities for grossular span the world. Gem material comes from Sri Lanka, Canada (Quebec), Switzerland, South Africa, Tanzania, Kenya, and East Africa.

Andradite is a brown or green garnet that commonly forms in limestones. Occasionally andradites are seen on the market, but usually they are cut for collectors only. An exception to this is the rare, desirable, and beautiful green gem of the variety known as demantoid. Demantoids are extremely scarce and in constant demand by collectors of rare gems. Melanite is a black andradite that contains titanium. Topazolite is an attractive yellow andradite variety, found principally in Italy. Topazolite is lovely, but almost never used as a gem, because the crystals are too small to yield cut stones of practical size.

Spessartine from Brazil (l.) is usually some shade of orange, while grossular (below) displays a wide range of lovely colors.

Uvarovite is deep green in color. Transparent material suitable for cutting, however, is extremely rare, and only tiny cut gems exist. Crystals occur in various parts of the world, but large crystals with gem potential occur only in Finland and the U.S.S.R.

All of the garnets that occur in nature can be classified as one of these six major garnet species. Many color varieties, however, have been given special names that are widely used. Essonite, or hessonite, is orangy-brown or brownish-orange grossular. Large gems have been cut from crystals found at the Jeffrey Asbestos Mine at Asbestos, Quebec. Rhodolite is a garnet with a chemical composition between pyrope and almandine. Its color is violet-red or purple, the hue sometimes resembling that of amethyst. Good rhodolite is scarce and expensive compared to most other garnets. Localities include Brazil, Ceylon, and Africa, with some purple material known from Cowee Creek, North Carolina. "Transvaalite," or "Transvaal jade" is a name given to a massive form of grossular. This material, green in color. does bear a resemblance to jade, although its value is much inferior. Localities include South Africa and Canada. Massive white grossular, suitable for carving, has been found in Burma, associated with jadeite.

Almandine containing fibrous inclusions occurs in Idaho. When cut into cabochons this material produces four-rayed and six-rayed stars that make curious and attractive collector items, as well as beautiful gems.

The variety of garnet called rhodolite is rare and desirable, such as this 13.1-carat gem from Rhodesia (above). Quartz crystals from Arkansas (opp.) are familiar to mineral collectors.

Modern technology has produced a host of new and exotic crystalline materials designed chiefly for use in semi-conductor and laser work. Among these compounds are some materials that have the same basic atomic structure as the natural garnets. However, being laboratory products, they have chemical compositions that do not correspond to any garnets produced by nature. Some of these so-called "synthetic garnets" have optical properties that make them suitable for use as simulated diamonds. These are discussed on page 146.

Consumer Tips—Garnet is the birthstone for January, and inexpensive red garnets are plentiful and readily available. In spite of this, much birthstone jewelry features synthetic gems, either corundum or spinel, designed to resemble garnet. Since these synthetics have very little intrinsic value, it is worthwhile insisting on natural garnets if the possession of a natural gem is at all important to the buyer.

Grossular garnets in shades of yellow, orange, and green are rarely seen in the gem trade. For this reason untrained sales personnel may regard with suspicion such gems brought into a jewelry shop for evaluation or appraisal. The gem's owner should remember that such a task requires the talents of a trained gemologist, and not be upset by random opinions as to the lack of authenticity of a stone. A good example of this is the case of vanadium grossular, which could easily be mistaken for emerald. For someone who is unaware of the color range of natural garnets, it is hard to imagine that a gem of such rich and beautiful a green hue could be a garnet. The same could be true of yellow, orange, and colorless stones.

Many reddish garnets are called rhodolite in the gem trade, whereas they may actually be almandine or pyrope. Since a chemical analysis may be needed for certain identification, color is not a suitable criterion to establish a species or variety name for a given gem. If a high-price premium is attached to the stone because of its supposed identity, verification of this identity might be worthwhile before purchase.

Quartz Gems

Quartz is one of the most common minerals on earth. It occurs in measurable quantities in almost every type of rock exposed at the earth's surface. Most beach sands are composed of quartz grains that have been rounded by wave action and mixed with other mineral fragments.

Chemically quartz is a simple oxide of silicon, the two most common elements in the earth's crust. This material forms quite easily in a variety of geological environments. Quartz may crystallize from molten rocks in their final stages of solidification. It frequently deposits in mineralized veins, usually from dilute solution in superheated watery fluids. Quartz makes up a large part of most pegmatites, and is often found filling cavities and cracks in a wide variety of rock types. Quartz is a ubiquitous geological "cement" and welds together such rocks as sandstone.

If allowed to form in an open space, quartz forms magnificent crystals with well-developed external forms of great beauty. The huge range of possible geological conditions in which quartz can crystallize allows for the existence of many external crystal shapes, making quartz popular among mineral collectors. To the gem lover, however, the interesting thing about quartz is the range of lovely colors it acquires,

and the panorama of interesting inclusions it displays.

Pure quartz is colorless. It was used as ornamental material as early as the Stone Age, and by the time of ancient Rome it was known that a wedge of quartz could be used as a lens to concentrate the sun's rays. Roman women carried small spheres of colorless quartz to cool their hands in the heat of the day. In modern times quartz has acquired many uses, most notably the control of radio frequencies. The millions of "crystal sets" made during World War II contained a thin slice of quartz in their tuning circuits. Quartz's valuable electrical properties make it useful in such devices as phonographs. More recently quartz has been used in the manufacture of accurate watches. Its optical properties make it valuable for use in special lens systems and prisms. Colorless quartz, to the jeweler, is rock crystal, a material with many gem uses. It can be faceted for wear, as well as carved into a variety of decorative objects.

Sometimes quartz forms in an environment where it incorporates millions of tiny bubbles and fluid inclusions, giving the material a white or "milky" appearance. Gold veins are often filled with milky quartz. This form of quartz has little gemological use.

Smoky quartz, however, is a popular gem material. The cause of the color is not fully understood, but is believed due to the action of radioactivity. Very dark smoky quartz is known as morion. Gems from Scotland were known as cairngorm (after the Cairngorm Mountains), although the supply from this source is now essentially exhausted. Today fine smoky quartz comes from the Swiss Alps, Brazil, Japan, Colorado, Maine, North Carolina, and California.

Citrine is yellow quartz, and the color may grade into a smoky brown. The color is due to the presence of iron, though some lemon-yellow quartz on the market derives its color from irradiation, and is not naturally colored. The primary source of citrine is Brazil. The color range of citrine is very similar to that of precious topaz. This has led to widespread misuse of the terms "citrine topaz" and "quartz topaz," both of which are quartz. Much of the golden-colored or brownish

The various colors of quartz include green, rose, and colorless (above). Gradations of color are seen in smoky quartz (opp. top), yellow citrine (mid.), purple amethyst (btm.), and even within amethyst crystals such as these from Vera Cruz, Mexico (r.).

quartz being sold today as "topaz" is actually heat-treated amethyst. Lighter-colored stones are sold as "Palmyra topaz" and deeper, reddish-brown gems as "Madeira topaz," both of which are misnomers.

Rose quartz occurs in a delicate pink color. The material is seldom completely transparent, but rather tends to be somewhat cloudy. The color ranges from nearly white to a deep rose-pink. Rose quartz is less common than other color varieties, and occurs chiefly in the cores of pegmatites. Occasionally inclusions of rutile are dense enough to create a weak star. The finest rose quartz comes from Brazil, the Malagasay Republic, Maine, and the U.S.S.R.

Green quartz is quite rare, but in the early 1950's it was discovered that certain amethysts, when heated, would turn a lovely green color. Such gems are met occasionally in the gem trade, sometimes marketed as prasiolite.

Amethyst is the most highly prized quartz variety. Its color range is from pale lilac (almost colorless) to a deep, rich, royal purple, sometimes showing reddish highlights. The growth of amethyst crystals is generally marked by changes in the composition of the growth solutions, leading to color zoning or banding in the crystals. Most cut amethysts display

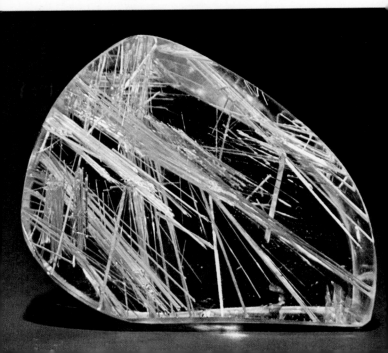

such banding, but the gem has to be turned in just the right position for this to be seen. The name "amethyst" comes from the Greek "amethustos," meaning "not drunken." In ancient times it was believed that an amethyst wearer could never become intoxicated. The gem was highly prized, and was used in both the breastplate of the High Priest of Israel and the foundation walls of the New Jerusalem. Amethyst has long been popular in ecclesiastical jewelry. Catherine the Great's love of amethyst helped develop sources in the U.S.S.R. and enriched the Russian Treasury. Some fine gems still adorn the British Crown Jewels. Massive chunks of amethyst, usually banded with white quartz, are carved into decorative objects and goblets. So-called "Siberian amethyst" once referred to Russian material, but it is a term now generally synonymous with a particularly fine color grade.

The hardness of quartz is 7 on the Mohs scale, so the material is hard enough for use in all types of jewelry. The mineral is fairly tough and has no cleavage, so gems wear well in rings. Most quartz gems are inexpensive, especially the colorless and rose and other pale colors. Citrines may command prices of several dollars per carat, and amethysts of large size and fine color may well cost several tens of dollars per carat.

Quartz with Inclusions

Many popular gems are quartz varieties containing various inclusions. These inclusions are actually minerals that formed along with the quartz, or else were present beforehand and became trapped inside the quartz crystals that grew around them. The list of observed inclusions in quartz includes dozens of mineral species, but only a few of them characterize material of gem significance.

65

Milky quartz from Zacatecas, Mexico (above)
may form spectacular crystals. Rutilated quartz (opp.)
from Brazil provides interesting and beautiful gems.

Rutilated quartz, sometimes called sagenite, contains inclusions of golden or reddish rutile. Some sagenites contain fibrous inclusions of epidote, actinolite, or other minerals, but rutile in long needle-like crystals is the most common. The finest such material comes from Brazil.

Tourmaline in quartz takes the form of black, rod-like crystals. Faceted gems are curiosities and highly decorative.

Dendritic quartz is so named because of the presence of tree-like inclusions. These are confined to thin layers within the quartz and produce interesting effects. The dendrites are actually deposits of minerals, such as manganese oxides, that precipitated along thin fractures within the quartz.

Aventurine is a rock made up of interlocked grains of quartz, containing small crystals of the mineral mica. In some varieties the mica is a green chrome-rich mineral called fuchsite, which colors the quartz a rich green. The mica flakes tend to be oriented in parallel and reflection from the myriad flakes produces a sparkling sheen. Most of the green aventurine seen in jewelry comes from India.

Tiger's-eye, or **tigereye,** is a popular and curious material. It consists of compact fibers of quartz that has replaced asbestos fibers. The light reflected from the fibers produces a strong sheen or silky appearance,

66

Silica assumes many forms, including aventurine (from India, above l.), tigereye (from Africa, top & btm. r.), various banded and patterned agates (opp. l.), and snowflake obsidian (from Utah, r.)

'like that of the original asbestos, known as chatoyancy. Sometimes variation in the color density of the material produces a "cat's-eye" effect, but more often the appearance is that of shimmering bands of light. Tigereye may vary in color from brown and brownish-yellow to blue and blue-green. The latter hues are generally referred to as hawk's-eye or falcon's-eye. Tigereye may be bleached in hydrochloric acid and dyed various colors, including red, yellow, gray, blue, and green. These are attractive colors but do not occur naturally. Heating yellow-brown tigereye can sometimes oxidize the iron that causes the brown coloration, producing reddish tones.

Quartz sometimes displays a cat's-eye effect caused by fibrous inclusions. Colors of such stones are generally grayish, black, gray-brown, greenish-yellow, and olive-green. The eye effect in quartz is sharper than in tigereye, but such gems are not as frequently seen in the gem trade.

Chalcedony

Quartz commonly forms as tiny grains or fibrous crystals, which may become packed together and stained various colors by natural pigments. This produces an enormous variety of patterns, color banding effects, and wispy inclusions in a translucent matrix. Such material is known as cryptocrystalline (microscopically crystallized) quartz, and the colored gem varieties are called agate and jasper. The basic crypto-crystalline matrix is called chalcedony.

Chalcedony occurs throughout the world and is one of the most common and least expensive of all gem materials. Agate was known to primitive man, and acquired a cloak of superstition. It was supposed to cure insomnia, breed prudence and caution, and bring its owner strength and victory in battle. Engraved and intricately worked chalcedony tools were made thousands of years before the birth of Christ.

Chalcedony is hard (7 on the Mohs scale), tough, and durable. Its fine grain allows for intricate and detailed carving and design. The various colored and patterned varieties have all been given individual names, and have distinctive histories.

Carnelian, the modern spelling of the older "cornelian," was immensely popular in ancient Egypt and among Mohammedans. The color, ranging from light brownish-red to deep clear red, is due to the presence of iron. Wax does not easily adhere to polished carnelian, which made this material useful for seals. Natural carnelian comes from Brazil, Uruguay, India, and California.

Chrysoprase is a highly translucent, apple-green chalcedony that is frequently mistaken for jade. It is the most valuable of the chalcedonies, colored green by traces of nickel silicate. Chrysoprase, usually cut into cabochons, beads, or cameos and intaglios, was popular in the Victorian era. Much of the "green onyx" and so-called chrysoprase sold today is dyed chalcedony. Fine natural chrysoprase comes from the Ural Mountains, California, Brazil, and Australia.

Prase is translucent yellow-green chalcedony, with little gem application.

Plasma is dark-green chalcedony with little translucency, sometimes with white or yellow spots. Occasionally iron minerals produce red or brownish spots, giving rise to the name "bloodstone" or "heliotrope."

Jasper is a catch-all term applied to opaque, colored chalcedonies. Often jasper displays no pattern, but the body coloration is usually heavy and rich, in shades of brown, red, green, and yellow. The material is dense and hard, and takes a high polish. Related materials, usually gray or black in color, are chert and flint. A pale, reddish chert with inclusions of colorless quartz is commonly dyed blue and sold as "Swiss lapis" or "German lapis," but these are not the same as lapis lazuli (see pages 103–104).

Agate is chalcedony in which the coloration takes the form of bands or wispy inclusions. Fortification agate contains straight or concentric bands, while moss agate displays colored or black mineral inclusions that create fanciful landscapes and images in the chalcedony matrix. Agates, like jaspers, occur throughout the world. The tremendous variety of patterns has led to a wealth of names, many of them for specific localities. The finest moss agates come from India, and from Montana, Oregon, Idaho, and Wyoming. Agates from Arizona, South Dakota, Mexico, and Brazil are known throughout the world. The variety of patterns and colors is almost endless.

Much commercial material is actually dyed chalcedony. Sard is basically like carnelian, but tends to be more brownish and somewhat

darker. Sardonyx consists of bands of sard, alternating with black and white layers. Onyx is black and white banded chalcedony. Black onyx commonly sold today is generally artificially blackened chalcedony. Brightly colored "onyx" in shades of red, blue, green, and yellow is dyed.

Chalcedony dissolved in circulating groundwater may replace buried wood and vegetation. The replacement is so slow and delicate that even the cell structure of the original wood is sometimes preserved. Petrified wood, most notably from Arizona, can be very colorful, and entire petrified trunk and limb sections make interesting curiosities. Another name for massive silicon oxide is silica, and wood replaced by chalcedony is sometimes called silicified wood.

Most of the chalcedonies are cut as cabochons or polished slabs, sometimes in unusual or fanciful forms. Chalcedony is ideal for carving and engraving, fashioning into beads, spheres, and bowls, and for making paperweights, pen holders, bookends, and boxes. Huge quantities of agate and jasper are tumble-polished for use in inexpensive jewelry.

The city of Idar-Oberstein in West Germany has been an important gem-cutting center since the year 31 A.D. The entire city is dedicated to the art of gem cutting and carving, and houses some of the great gem craftsmen of the world. German cutting has become synonymous with high quality. A variety of materials is cut, but the chalcedonies occupy a place of tremendous importance in the area of large-volume low-cost gems.

69

Orbicular jasper from California (top l.), "Owyhee jasper" from Oregon (top r.), "Bruneau jasper" from Idaho (btm. l.), and a lovely patterned jasper from Utah (btm. r.).

Opal

Opal has been called the Queen of Gems. Few descriptions are adequate to describe the finest opals: a white, snowy landscape dotted with fireflies of red, gold, blue, purple, and green; a black night streaked with rainbow lightning; the aurora borealis captured in stone. Mysterious, elusive, varied, and delicate, opal has been treasured since ancient times for its unique properties and beauty.

Opal is silicon oxide, and thus closely related to chalcedony. But while chalcedony is just silica, opal contains a variable amount of water in its structure. Opal is softer than quartz gems, about 5½ to 6½ on the Mohs scale, and is much more fragile and brittle than chalcedony. But what makes opal distinctive is its unique play of color, called "fire."

Most opal is dull and lifeless, and so-called "common opal" tends to be gray or yellowish, occasionally waxy looking and translucent. Once in a great while a piece is found transparent enough to facet. Otherwise common opal has little or no gem value. Unlike quartz, which forms good crystals, opal is more like a hardened jelly, or "gel."

There are four types of gem opal:

White opal is opaque, white material that looks much like porcelain. The colors appear as flashes, speckles, or sheets of rainbow colors. White opals are the kind most commonly seen in opal jewelry.

Black opal also contains fire, but the body color is dark gray or black. This accentuates the color play, producing a dramatic effect. Black opals are extremely rare and costly.

Water opal is transparent, colorless opal that contains brilliant flashes of color swimming within it.

Fire opal is transparent or translucent opal with an orange or red body color. It may or may not display fire. The term "fire opal" is frequently misused. Opal that has a color play is called precious opal. The color play itself is called fire. Fire opals are simply reddish or orange opals, usually turbid, that may not have any fire!

The ancient Romans had a passion for fine opals, and the Senator Nonius had one coveted by Marc Antony. Nonius was forced to choose either giving up the gem or exile from Rome; he chose the latter. This esteem of opal continued until the 17th Century, but afterward lost popularity. Part of this is connected with the superstition of opal as a "hard luck" stone. This attitude may have been caused in part by a novel by Sir Walter Scott called "Anne of Geierstein," in which an opal played a malevolent role. Sales of opals dropped drastically after publication of this book, and did not fully revive until the present time. A major part of the "bad luck" reputation is probably due to the tendency

of opal to crack spontaneously.

By far the finest and most treasured opals come from Australia. Some Australian opals are so spectacular that they were given individual names, such as the Empress, the Red Admiral, the Pandora, Light of the World, and the Harlequin Prince. White opal may sell for a few dollars to several hundred dollars per carat. A fine black opal, however, can command more than $1,000 per carat.

Gem quality opal comes from Honduras, though Honduran opal is not commercially significant today. Czechoslovakia was the source of Roman opal, especially the town of Czerwenitza, which was formerly in Hungary and whose deposits were extensively mined before 1800. Mexico produces fine water opal and fire opal, sometimes with a striking color play. Fine precious opal comes from the Virgin Valley in Nevada, where the opal generally replaces wood and animal bones, in the manner of petrified wood. In recent years a quantity of white precious opal from Brazil has been marketed. This material, some of it rivaling the best Australian white opal, is more heat resistant and less brittle than Australian white opal.

Terms sometimes applied to gem opal are harlequin (a mosaic of angular patches of fire); flame opal (regular color bands or streaks); gold **71**

*Opal triplets from Australia can be large
and spectacular, as is this 30 x 23mm oval gem
(top) that resembles a fine black opal.*

opal (the whole surface of which glows with a golden sheen); girasol (a wave of blue light on a transparent background); opal-onyx, a material built up of alternating layers of common opal and precious opal.

Frequently, as in the case of opal-onyx, opal is mined that is essentially devoid of fire, but contains a very thin layer of precious opal. This can be exposed by careful cutting, but if the layer is in a thin seam of white opal there may not be enough support left to yield a stone that can be used in jewelry. The answer to this problem is to cement the opal layer to a backing material to give it thickness and strength. The most common backing materials are common opal (called potch), onyx, and a ceramic material. The resulting two-layer sandwich is called a doublet; the cement used between the layers is usually blackened to accentuate the colors in the thin, precious opal layer. From the top a doublet looks like a fine black opal, even though the precious opal used is white opal. But the opal layer on a doublet is still exposed to wear, and can suffer damage if not cared for.

In recent years this problem has also been solved by the creation of the triplet. This is a doublet, on top of which is cemented a cabochon of colorless quartz. The quartz adds additional thickness to the stone, prevents damage in setting, and protects the opal layer from wear. In addition, the quartz cabochon has the effect of a magnifying glass, enlarging the color play and giving more of the appearance of fine black opal.

Opal doublets and triplets are sold by the stone, rather than by the carat. The largest available triplets have diameters measured in inches and may cost several hundred dollars. Small stones can be purchased for under $100.

72   Opal is not a common gemstone, although non-precious varieties

Hyalite opal, such as this 5.15-carat Mexican stone (above), is rarely faceted. More commonly seen are fire opal and jelly opal from Mexico (opp.), usually cut into cabochons.

abound. Prices have risen to the point where synthesis became an enticing goal. Recently Pierre Gilson of Paris has succeeded in synthesizing in the laboratory both white and black opal of fine quality. The synthetics are very difficult to tell from natural opal, and are sure to play a major role in the gem market in the years ahead.

Consumer Tips—Black opal is the most expensive opal, and fine gems may bring more than $1,000 per carat. Fine white opals may sell for hundreds of dollars per carat. Doublets and triplets are usually sold by the stone, rather than by weight, and are usually cut to "standard" millimeter dimensions.

The opal in doublets and triplets is *not* black opal, but rather a thin layer of white opal with black cement behind it. The overall effect strongly resembles fine black opal.

Any opal may spontaneously develop a network of fine internal cracks. The tendency for this to happen is called crazing, and some people believe that perpetual soaking or storage of opals in water or mineral oil will prevent it. Opal is silicon dioxide with a small, variable amount of water in its structure. The gradual loss of this water is the apparent cause of spontaneous crazing. Crazing is not characteristic of much of the black opal from Australia, although it is prevalent in opal from the Virgin Valley, Nevada. Doublets and triplets do not tend to craze, probably because of the constricting action of the adhering cement.

Opal is a very poor ringstone, because of its softness and fragility. Triplets are far superior to solid opals in rings, because the quartz top of a triplet imparts strength and hardness. An opal ring should be purchased with the thought that it will not stand rough treatment. Opal is far more suitable for pins and pendants.

Topaz

In ancient times, just about any yellow gem was likely to be called topaz. The name itself may have been derived from a Sanskrit word meaning "fire." The association of topaz and the color yellow is unfortunate, since fine topaz occurs in colorless crystals, as well as pink, blue, green, and a pleasing "sherry" color.

The jewelry trade has created a host of terms for the sale of yellow gems. For example, we find "smoky topaz," which is actually smoky quartz; "citrine topaz," "Bohemian topaz," and "occidental topaz," which are all citrine; "Oriental topaz," which is yellow corundum. Most of the stones sold as "topaz" today are actually citrine. True topaz is labeled properly with only two modifying terms: "precious" and "Imperial," the latter referring to a Brazilian occurrence.

The most important color variety of topaz is the range of yellow and brown gems, mined chiefly at Ouro Preto, Brazil. Some of this material actually attains a bright-red hue. Golden-brown topaz is the most expensive color variety, with large faceted gems commanding prices of several hundred dollars per carat.

Related to the brownish stones is pink topaz, because it has been found that some sherry-colored and yellow material will turn pink on heating. True pink topaz does occur in nature, but is extremely rare. A rare light-violet topaz color has also been observed.

Colorless topaz is both attractive and inexpensive. Proper cutting

can yield bright and sparkling gems, but the lack of color reduces its demand and keeps its price low. Blue topaz, on the other hand, has become increasingly popular. This is partly due to the surge in popularity of aquamarine. Fine aquamarine has become so expensive and scarce that blue topaz has begun to find wide use as a substitute. Most blue topaz is fairly pale, but some material can apparently be turned a deep color by irradiation with gamma rays. Green and greenish-yellow gems are occasionally seen in the gem trade, but these are rare and not generally known to the buying public. There is currently no effective distinguishing test for irradiated blue topaz or heat-treated pink topaz. Purchase of such stones should always be accompanied by some statement indicating natural origin or prior treatment.

Topaz usually forms late in the crystallization of rocks. It is typically found in pegmatite dikes, and crystals can reach enormous size. Golden-brown crystals up to a foot in length are known, but even these are dwarfed by the 100-pound behemoths found in Brazilian deposits. Some of these crystals are perfectly formed and nearly completely transparent.

Topaz is very hard, 8 on the Mohs scale, so it wears well in jewelry. Its only drawback is a well-developed cleavage, making the cutting of topaz gems a tricky business. A casual blow to a cut topaz could cause it to split, so rings should be treated with some care. Topaz takes a high **75**

Collectors prize topaz crystals from Utah (above), as well as the fine blue gems cut from Brazilian crystals. This one (opp.) weighs 54.4 carats and is of museum quality.

polish and makes a spectacular jewelry stone. Its specific gravity is much higher than the typical quartz imitations, so unset stones are fairly easy to distinguish just on the basis of "heft."

Some topaz tends to fade in sunlight. This is especially true of pale-brown material from the U.S.S.R. and Mexico, as well as from Japan and the Thomas Range, Utah. Sometimes irradiated stones will also bleach out in sunlight, but the dark-blue material seems to be fairly stable.

Topaz occurs in many localities throughout the world. Brazil is the chief supplier of colorless, pale-sherry, and blue varieties. Ouro Preto, Brazil is the world's chief source of fine golden and yellow topaz. Mining is a hand operation, and the total output per day is quite small, contributing to the scarcity of these stones.

Fine blue and greenish crystals come from the Ural Mountains, U.S.S.R., and these are avidly sought by collectors. Colorless, yellow, and sherry-colored topaz is found in San Luis Potosi and Durango, Mexico. Good crystals come from Japan, the Malagasay Republic, Ireland, Rhodesia, Nigeria, and, in the United States, Colorado, Maine, New Hampshire, and Utah. Topaz is abundant in the gem gravels of

The most familiar topaz color is yellow or orange (above), chiefly from Brazil. Colorless crystals from Japan (r.) are collector items, and gems in a wide range of colors (opp.) are available.

Burma and Sri Lanka, where it is recovered as a by-product in the mining of ruby and sapphire.

Topaz has not been synthesized in the laboratory on a commercial basis. So-called "synthetic topaz" is actually synthetic corundum that has been made in a suitable color.

Consumer Tips—The most frequently misused terms in the gem trade include "smoky topaz," "citrine topaz," and related names. These are tradenames devised by jewelry sellers to sell quartz, a common, inexpensive gem material, as topaz, a fairly rare, costly gem with optical properties superior to those of quartz. Loose gems of topaz and quartz can easily be distinguished on the basis of heft (the topaz has a much higher specific gravity) and brilliance (topaz has a higher refractive index). Set stones, especially when small, can be difficult or impossible to distinguish with the naked eye.

In purchasing a yellow stone labeled "topaz" the buyer should *always* insist on verification and guarantee of the authenticity and natural origin of the stone. Suspicion should be aroused if a "topaz" ring containing a large yellow-orange stone is priced at only $100 or $200. If the stone is precious topaz, its value might be more than $100 *per carat,* exclusive of the setting.

Blue topaz has appeared on the gem market in increasing quantities. This is largely due to the escalating price of aquamarine, and the need for an inexpensive, natural blue gem on the marketplace. To many jewelers, however, the material is sufficiently new that a customer bringing a blue topaz to a shop for evaluation might be met with the comment "that can't be topaz, there is no such thing as blue topaz." This problem will diminish as more blue topaz is seen in the jewelry trade.

Topaz, although listed as the birthstone for November, is seldom seen except in the larger jewelry shops. This is a shame, because in white and pale colors topaz may cost only a few dollars per carat. There is enough such material available to make distribution possible on a much wider scale than currently seen.

Jade

To many people jade and the color green are synonymous. The word brings to mind the fabled past of ancient China, the opulence of Oriental Emperors. In fact, the Chinese worked a material they called "yu" as early as 1000 B.C. Today we know this material as jade. The name of the gem itself, however, is derived from the Spanish name "piedra de Hijada," or "stone of the loins." Cortes and his conquistadores brought back to Spain many pieces of jade, which they found to be in widespread use among the Indians of Central America.

The term "jade" actually refers to two distinct and different minerals: jadeite and nephrite. Jadeite is sodium aluminum silicate; nephrite is a calcium magnesium silicate. The name nephrite comes from the belief that polished jade pebbles that sometimes resemble kidneys would help cure kidney disorders. Thus, the name "kidney stone," Latinized to "lapis nephriticus," eventually was shortened to "nephrite." Nephrite occurs in various colors, including greenish-gray (the so-called "mutton-fat jade"), brown, and dark green. The hardness is 6½ on the Mohs scale, but the physical structure of the material is that of many interlocked crystals. Thus, nephrite is extremely tough. Nephrite is also sometimes called greenstone.

Jadeite consists of interlocked grains, but in jadeite these are more granular than fibrous, so jadeite surfaces often have a "dimpled" appearance. The hardness of jadeite is 7 on the Mohs scale, making it slightly harder than nephrite and providing one distinguishing test.

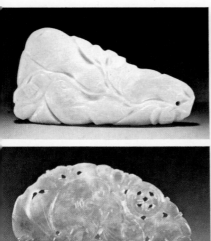

Jadeite occurs in an enormous range of colors: white, pink, lilac, brown, red, orange, blue, black, and many shades of green. A single piece of jadeite will frequently display several colors, with subtle changes of hue and shade in different parts of the piece. The most highly valued color is a rich green resembling that of the finest emerald. Translucent stones of this superb color, generally known as "Imperial jade," may sell for several thousand dollars per carat. The color range for jadeite is much greater than that for nephrite. A black or dark-green jadeite that contains large quantities of iron oxide is called chloromelanite.

Nephrite has been used to make tools, weapons, and ornaments, and played a central role in the religious rites of many primitive peoples, including the Chinese, the Central American Aztecs, and the Maoris of New Zealand. Ancient jade that has been buried for some time, appropriately called "buried jade," is of great interest to archaeologists.

The major commercial source of fine jadeite is Burma. The material is difficult to mine because of its great toughness. In times past the preferred method was to heat the jade outcroppings and then cool them suddenly with cold water, the thermal "shock" being sufficient to crack up the jade for easy removal. Today, drills and other more modern techniques are used. Boulders of jade that have lain exposed for some time acquire a brownish "skin" due to weathering. The Chinese carvers were specialists in making use of this skin.

The material worked by the ancient Chinese was apparently nephrite from Central Asia. Jadeite was not known in China before the 18th Century. It was long conjectured that a source of jade existed in Central America, possibly Mexico or Guatemala. Jade was finally discovered in Guatemala in 1954, thus confirming a source for Pre-Columbian material. Jadeite, in the form of stream boulders, occurs in southern California in several locations. This material displays various colors, including grayish-green, pale green, bluish-green, and white.

Nephrite occurs in many parts of the world. China is an ancient source. Green nephrite comes from eastern Siberia, and the occurrence at Lake Baikal is well known. Material from another Russian source, near Irkutsk, contains black specks of graphite that make the material very distinctive. Nephrite from New Zealand is termed "Maori stone," "New Zealand greenstone," and "Axestone"; it occurs in stream beds as flattened pebbles easily fashioned into weapons. This material is primarily dark green in color. Pale-colored nephrite has been found in Poland; other European occurrences include Italy and Germany. Jade is found in Alaska and in British Columbia. Nephrite from Lander, Wyoming has attained great popularity in recent years. This is a distinctive material, generally mottled green and white in appearance. Nephrite localities also include Washington, Mexico, Brazil, Rhodesia, and Taiwan. **79**

Jade occurs in many colors, including yellow (opp. top l.),
as well as the familiar green shade (btm. l.). Fine blocks showing
several colors have been intricately carved (opp. r.).

Jade is a difficult stone to cut and polish and posed great problems for cutters in primitive societies. It may have required years just to slice through large boulders using a rope "saw" and sand as an abrasive. Generations may have worked on a single, intricate carving, using pieces of stone or bamboo, water, and sand to fashion intricate and detailed curves and figures. It is truly remarkable that such primitive tools and techniques could have produced the delicate and highly polished vases, carvings, and brush pots that we see in museums today.

True jade needs no modifying adjectives in its name, and stands on its own merits. Many inferior materials, however, have been named using the word "jade" as a suffix, in hopes of adding value through inference. *All* of the following are tradenames and should be abandoned in time, but are included here for reference.

"Korea jade" is bowenite, a hard variety of the mineral serpentine. "Transvaal jade" is actually a massive variety of green grossular garnet. "Amazon jade" is green microcline feldspar. "Indian jade" is aventurine, a massive quartz colored by inclusions of green mica. "American jade" or "Californite" is a mixture of two green minerals, idocrase and grossular. "Australian jade" is chrysoprase, a lovely green silica mineral. "Colorado jade" is also green microcline, and "jasper jade" is green jasper. "Fukien jade," "Manchurian jade," and "Honan jade" are all sopastone. "Mexican jade" is a green-dyed marble or calcite. "Oregon jade" is a dark-green jasper. "Silver peak jade" is malachite, a green copper mineral. Other jade imitations include green glass, white jade that has been stained or dyed purple or green; green marble called Verd Antique; various other green minerals. This list is not complete, since many local tradenames are undoubtedly in use.

Consumer Tips—Many materials strongly resemble jade, especially serpentine and bowenite, and nephrite and jadeite may frequently resemble each other. Identification of a carving or jewelry item may require sophisticated laboratory tests; visual checking may be satisfactory much of the time, in the hands of a true expert who has handled a tremendous amount of jade, but even experts can be fooled. The value of a piece may depend heavily on the identity of the material from which it is made.

Dyes are frequently added to jade to deepen or change the color. White jadeite is frequently stained green or pale purple to mimic the so-called "mauve jade." The process can usually be detected in a gem laboratory, but not by eye.

A gemstone may be one of a huge variety of colors and still be jade. The misconception that jade has to be green is prevalent, but may disappear in time. However, authentication and identification should be entrusted only to a specialist.

Tourmaline crystals from Brazil (opp. l.) provide much of today's gem material. The blue variety, indicolite (btm. r.), is popular, while brown gems from Africa (top r.) are less frequently seen. Green tourmaline (center) is the most familiar to gem buyers.

Tourmaline

Tourmaline, a gem not widely known to gem buyers, displays the most dazzling and surpassing variety of colors of all known gemstones. Some crystals may display two or three color bands along their length, or show complex concentric zoning in cross section. Some of the most delicate, subtle, and exquisite colors in the mineral kingdom belong to the tourmaline group.

Tourmaline is actually a general group term that applies to several minerals with similar atomic structures and chemical compositions. Confusion sometimes arises because there are mineral species names (elbaite, schorl, and dravite) and names for color varieties: rubellite (pink and red), indicolite (blue), achroite (colorless), siberite (reddish-violet), and dravite (brown).

Tourmaline has no cleavage, and therefore doesn't tend to break or chip easily. Its hardness is 7–7½ on the Mohs scale. The color range is vast. In fact, the name tourmaline comes from the ancient Singhalese word "turamali," meaning "mixed precious stones." The implication is that Ceylonese gem dealers could not identify various gemstones, many of which were undoubtedly tourmalines.

The most valuable tourmalines are red, with a tinge of purple or violet. The finest of these come from Maine, California, and Brazil. The gradation in hue among the reddish tourmalines is almost infinite, involving mixtures of red, brown, violet, pink, and orange. African stones tend to be pink with a tinge of brown, while gems from Maine and Brazil are rich violet-red. California tourmalines are a distinctive "shocking" pastel pink.

Green tourmalines are modified by shades of blue, yellow, and brown. Crystals may be so dark in color as to be virtually black. The finest green tourmalines resemble top quality emeralds, but this color is extremely rare and highly desired. By far the majority of green tourmalines are mined in Brazil. A variety rich in chromium may sell for more than $100 per carat. The green hues blend imperceptibly into blue-green, but pure-blue tourmaline is quite rare. Lilac-colored stones are occasionally found. Large blue gems may command high prices. Colorless, yellow, and orange tourmalines are quite rare and seldom seen in gem form.

Color-zoned crystals are sometimes cut for jewelry use. Of great popularity are the concentrically banded crystal sections that are almost always pink in the center and green on the outside. These have been fancifully named "watermelon tourmaline," and polished crystal slices are worn as earrings and pendants. Crystals that change color along their length are called "bicolor" or "multicolored" tourmalines.

82   Sometimes a tourmaline crystal contains enough fibrous or tube-like

Cat's-eye tourmalines from Brazil (top l.) often display sharp "eyes." California rubellite (top r.), this one 21.3 carats, is bright pink. African tourmalines (btm.) occur in many colors.

inclusions to display a chatoyant sheen. When cut into cabochons such material yields interesting "cat's-eye tourmalines." These are found in various colors, most commonly green and pink. Another interesting tourmaline variety shows a color change resembling that of alexandrite: yellowish-green in daylight and reddish-orange in artificial light.

Tourmaline occurs in pegmatites, often associated with other gem minerals. Tourmaline frequently forms with quartz, and crystal groups of tourmaline perched on large quartz clusters are desired by collectors. Localities throughout the world are numerous, but gem material is less widely distributed. Sri Lanka may well have been the first source of this gem, and still produces waterworn pebbles of fine material in shades of yellow and brown. Most of the world's tourmaline today comes from the state of Minas Gerais, Brazil in a wide variety of colors. Some Brazilian crystals can reach enormous size, several feet in length, but such crystals are seldom of gem quality. Fine gem tourmaline comes from the Malagasay Republic, South West Africa, Rhodesia, and Mozambique. In the United States, Maine and California are the most notable sources of tourmaline. Recently discovered deposits at Newry, Maine have yielded fine crystals with a high percentage of gem material, including some of the finest red and blue-green stones in the world. Pala, California is a well-known source of fine pink tourmaline.

The dichroism of tourmaline is very strong, and crystals are usually cut with the table parallel to the length of the crystal.

Consumer Tips—Tourmaline is available in the trade in large quantities and in a huge array of colors, yet it seems less well known than other gems. Tourmalines are hard and durable and make fine ringstones, especially when set with small diamonds. The price ranges from a few dollars per carat to more than $300 per carat, with large, flawless gems commanding the premium prices. Brazil produces most of the green and blue-green gems seen on the market, but occasional stones from other sources may be available at certain times and places.

Color determines price among tourmalines; the most desirable colors are a green resembling the color of fine emerald, characteristic of chrome-tourmaline, and lively pale-green shades, as well as the rich reddish-pink of fine rubellite. Flawed stones of any color are less desirable and less expensive than "clean" stones, except in the case of California rubellite and bicolored and tricolored gems. These latter are almost never completely free of inclusions or minor internal flaws.

Synthetic gems created to resemble tourmaline cannot be distinguished easily with the naked eye. Such synthetics are commonly found in jewelry today, since tourmaline is the alternate birthstone for October. The authenticity of a tourmaline should therefore always be checked before purchase.

Feldspars

Moonstone, with its mysterious white or blue sheen, is one of the most familiar gem varieties of a large group of minerals called the feldspars.

Feldspars are the most abundant minerals in the crust of the earth. All are aluminum silicates containing calcium, sodium, or potassium. The potassium members include orthoclase and microcline. The other feldspars, forming the plagioclase group, have been classified according to the relative amount of calcium and sodium present. There are six minerals in this series which are, in sequence of increasing calcium content: albite, oligoclase, andesine, labradorite, bytownite, and anorthite.

Most of the feldspars have been cut as gems. Nearly all the plagioclases occasionally form transparent crystals that are faceted, but these are rare collector stones. The important feldspar gems tend to be translucent to nearly opaque and show interesting optical effects. All the feldspars have a Mohs hardness of 6–6½, which is relatively low for a gem. In addition, feldspars have good cleavages, so cut gems must be worn with some care.

Moonstone is the most popular and important microcline gem. Its blue or white sheen is called adularescence, and is caused by the presence of tiny crystals of albite arranged in layers within the host microcline. Moonstone may be completely transparent, and the sheen can be either silvery white or a soft but distinct blue, the latter being highly prized. The adularescent sheen resembles a cloud of light that appears within the gem when it is turned at the right angle to the eye.

Some moonstones are nearly opaque and may have a strong body color, which may be beige, pink, green, yellow, white, gray, or brown. These are usually cut as high-domed cabochons, and the sheen is concentrated at the top in a bright spot that sometimes extends across the stone as a distinct "eye." Such gems have been called "cat's-eye moonstones." Some others may have a second ray at right angles to the first, forming a cross. Moonstones with a strong body color are primarily from India. The most important historical sources for fine moonstone are Sri Lanka and upper Burma. Other sources include Canada, Switzerland, Brazil, Australia, California, Virginia, and Colorado. Mining is usually carried out by hand, and stones are frequently cut locally. Moonstone is still considered a sacred gem in India and it has been used in jewelry there for centuries.

Orthoclase makes a very attractive faceted gem, especially material with a rich golden-yellow color. The finest such material comes from the Malagasay Republic, sometimes in huge crystals. Cut stones weighing several hundred carats are exhibited in major museums. Orthoclase

Orthoclase from the Malagasay Republic, 22.8 and 7.75 carats (l.). Labradorite (below l.) displays a bright iridescence, and amazonite from Colorado (below r.) is a rich blue-green.

is a lovely gem, but too scarce to have become commercially popular, so it remains a collector's stone.

Microcline is considered a gem when it exhibits a distinct bluish or bluish-green color, to which the name "amazonite" or "amazonstone" has been applied. Generally this material is cut into cabochons and beads, since it is inexpensive (several dollars per pound in the rough) and fairly durable. Amazonite has become popular among gem hobbyists. Good material comes from Brazil, India, Amelia Court House, Virginia, and Pike's Peak, Colorado. Other localities include Tanzania, Canada, and the U.S.S.R.

Sunstone is a type of albite or bytownite that has a golden-brown body color. Its sheen is like that of moonstone, except that it is gold colored and tends to concentrate at the top of a cabochon. Albite with a white iridescence is called peristerite. Sometimes albite contains inclusions or flakes of a metallic mineral that produce a "spangled" reflection as the stone is turned.

Labradorite is the most popular and interesting plagioclase gem. This feldspar sometimes occurs in transparent yellow crystals from which lovely stones can be faceted. More commonly it forms crystalline masses with extensive internal twinning that produces many thin layers. Light interference from these layers produces a sheen or glow that sweeps across the entire stone. Sometimes the color is uniform over a **85**

large area, or it may break up into patches of different colors. These colors include blue, blue-green, green, yellow, and gold. Spectacular labradorite comes from Labrador, the U.S.S.R., and Canada.

Consumer Tips—Fine moonstone is not common, especially material displaying a blue, well-centered sheen, and fine sunstone is just as scarce. Faceted plagioclase gems are very rare and may vary in price with size and quality. Maximum prices for any cut feldspar would be a few tens of dollars per carat. With the exception of moonstone, few of the feldspars are used commercially, although they are widely used by hobbyists.

Careful study is required to determine the exact identity of a feldspar, since optical properties are similar and chemistry is the basic distinguishing feature. A questionable identification might therefore

86 have to be checked by a gem-testing laboratory.

Sunstones (top l.) make rare faceted gems. Amazonite (top r.) is often cut by hobbyists, as is labradorite with a blue sheen (btm.). Pearls (opp.) are generally graded according to size.

Pearl

To ancient man the natural forces around him inspired reverence and awe. The sun and moon were deities with formidable powers over the lives and destinies of men. The discovery of a glimmering, lustrous object from the sea that seemed to embody the glow of the full moon was undoubtedly the inspiration for a new cult. It is believed that pearls were known and esteemed 3,500 years before Christ. To the ancients the sea was the source of all life. And in the lands around the Mediterranean, a shell cult developed that brought such status to the pearl that it remained a Queen of Gems. No other gem has retained its level of value and position of desirability for as long a time.

The pearl is actually the response of a mollusk to the presence of an irritating impurity in its body. Saltwater pearls are found in non-edible oysters, and freshwater pearls in mussels (clams). The principal genus of oyster associated with saltwater pearls is Pinctada, and Unio is the primary freshwater pearl-producing clam genus. Many other types of mollusks produce concretions in their bodies, but few display the iridescence associated with gem pearls.

Within the two hinged shells of the Pinctada mollusks are various tissue layers. Mother-of-pearl is the layer to which the body parts are attached, lining the inside of the shell. If an irritating particle, such as a grain of sand, gets inside the shell, the mollusk's tissues will start to deposit a protective layer of nacre (mother-of-pearl) around it. This accretion may become a pearl. If the particle is enclosed completely by soft tissue, the pearl may be round and well formed. If the irritating particle becomes attached to the shell of the mollusk, a hemispherical-shaped blister pearl will result.

A pearl is built up in layers concentrically arranged around the irritant. The layers may consist of a mineral produced by the mollusk; but unless the outer layers consist of nacre, the pearl will not display the lustrous iridescence called orient that makes pearls so highly prized and beautiful. Edible oysters cannot manufacture the semi-transparent layers of nacre that are characteristic of gem pearls.

Below the orient, sometimes called overtone, is the body color or background color of the pearl. Overtone is seen in reflected light coming from the surface of the pearl, and its colors include purple, green, yellow, pink, and orange. Body color is subdivided into three basic colors: white, black, and "colored," including red, yellow, purple, violet, blue, and green. Black pearls include grays as well, plus bronze, dark blue, blue-green, and green pearls with metallic lusters. White pearls include cream-colored, light rose, and cream rose (both with pink overtones), and so-called "fancy" pearls which always have three colors: cream, rose, and a blue or green overtone.

Saltwater mollusks are the most important producers of pearls today, and by far the majority of the world natural pearl production is from the Persian Gulf, between Saudi Arabia and Iran. Only about one mollusk in 40 contains a pearl, and the total number of mollusks recovered tends to be small. From the Gulf the pearls travel to Bombay, where they are cleaned by immersion in hydrogen peroxide and by drying in the sun. After sorting and drilling, the finer grades are sold to Western dealers, and most of these pearls eventually appear in Paris and then the United States. Paris is a major distribution point for pearls. Bombay is essentially a brokerage center.

Fine pearls also come from Sri Lanka, Australia, Japan, Mexico, Panama, Venezuela, and Tahiti. Freshwater pearls are found in the Mississippi River and its tributaries, as well as Scotland and China.

The pearl trade employs a variety of tradenames. Among these are the following:

"Oriental pearls"—those found in saltwater mollusks of the Persian Gulf.

"Ceylon" or "Madras" pearls—fancy blue, green, or violet overtones on a white or cream base.

"Venezuela" pearls—white or yellow; more transparent than Oriental.

"Tahiti" pearls—white pearls with little overtone, sometimes with a grayish metallic cast.

"Australian" pearls—white with almost no overtone.

"Panama" pearls—usually black, grayish, or yellow.

"Freshwater" pearls—usually have strong colors and orient; fancy colors are common.

The shapes of pearls are classified as: round, pear shaped, egg

shaped, drop shaped (teardrop), button shaped, baroque shaped (all irregular shapes except other named shapes), slugs (baroque pearls but with poor luster), half-pearls (half of a round pearl), three-quarters pearls (three fourths round with a flat side), seed pearls (unsymmetrical and very small), dust pearls (too small to be used in jewelry), and blister pearls (attached to side of shell).

The value of a pearl is based on color, luster, translucency, texture, shape, and size. The finest have pure and even color; a strong overtone with a high luster; strong semi-translucency; no cracks, scratches, and dents or blemishes; round shape; large size. The value of a pearl is estimated by multiplying a base rate by the square of the weight, so small increases in size have a large effect on value. Large pearls that meet all the requirements for fine quality are extremely scarce and tremendously valuable. The appraising of pearls is even more complex than that of diamonds. Pearl rarity increases faster as sizes become larger than does diamond rarity. Only extensive training and considerable experience qualify a person to appraise pearls properly.

Pearls are available in various colors, as well as various sizes. Cultured pearls (above) are indistinguishable, by eye, from those of natural origin.

Cultured Pearls

The cultured pearl is basically a 20th-Century product. Several men tried to develop a method for producing spherical pearls, and the names Nishikawa, Mise, and Mikimoto are prominent in this regard. After a complicated patent settlement, Mikimoto emerged dominant in the cultured pearl industry.

A cultured pearl is produced by inserting a mother-of-pearl bead into the tissues of a pearl-producing mollusk. The mollusk treats the bead as an irritant and deposits a nacreous coating over it. Thus, the basic difference between a natural and a cultured pearl is the nature and size of the nucleus particle, and the way the pearl originates.

Blister pearls are produced by inserting a half-bead against the shell of the mollusk. After a layer of nacre has been deposited over the bead, the whole formation is cut out and the nacreous dome cemented onto a mother-of-pearl bead. The result is called a mabe pearl.

Biwa pearls are produced at Lake Biwa, Japan using freshwater clams. Biwa pearls are irregular in shape, but have good color and orient. They are distinctive because they have no nucleus; instead of a bead, small squares of tissue are inserted into the clam. The pearls that develop require three years to grow.

Japan is the world's leading producer of cultured pearls. The usual shapes produced are the baroque, round, button, oval, pear, and egg; very few cultured pearls are perfect spheres. Of all gems, pearls are the most difficult to authenticate. The only truly reliable test involves the use of an x-ray machine, which can be dangerous in unskilled hands. Fine cultured pearls are, to the eye, indistinguishable from genuine pearls, and simple tests are not reliable in all cases.

The qualities that determine the value of genuine pearls also apply in the case of cultured pearls. Generally prices of cultured pearls are lower, but even a strand of these may bring a price in excess of $100,000.

Organic Gems

Only a few of the materials we call gems are not of mineral origin. The so-called organic gems include pearls and mother-of-pearl, amber, coral, ivory, jet, and shell.

Amber

Amber is the hardened, fossilized resin or sap of ancient pine trees. Various species of pine trees produce different types of sap, so there are several types of amber with varying compositions. The material is usually amorphous and occurs in lumps displaying a resinous luster. The hardness is 2–2½ on the Mohs scale, so amber can easily be cut with a pocket knife. The specific gravity is very low, about 1.2, and amber will float in sea water. This is a good test for genuine amber, since most imitations will sink in a saturated water solution of salt. The low S.G. also allows amber, released from sediments, to be washed up on shore by wave action. Such pieces may be sand size or reach a weight of many pounds.

Amber can be dark brown to pale yellow, orange, red, whitish, greenish, bluish, or violetish. The most common colors are orange, yellow, and brown; the other colors are usually caused by light interference of bubbles of air inside the material. Natural amber is generally termed "block amber" and includes the following types: cloudy or bastard amber contains many small bubbles, fatty amber is translucent, also full of small bubbles and resembles fat; clear amber is transparent.

Some amber is mined, rather than recovered from seashores; this

Baltic amber (above) is a popular gem material and usually some shade of yellow or brown. Japanese worker (opp.) inserts nucleus of pig-toe-shell near mantle of living oyster.

has been termed "pit amber." So-called "bone amber" is opaque and soft, resembling bone or ivory. Exposure to sun and sea water may cause amber to turn opaque and chalky, with a "foamy" or frothy appearance.

Extensive deposits of amber are found on the shores of the Baltic Sea. Much amber is recovered at the shore, but considerable amounts are mined. The amber washed ashore is released at the sea bottom from the sediments in which it has been preserved. These sediments are millions of years old. Since amber sometimes contains the remains of insects that were trapped in the sticky tree sap of an ancient pine tree, we may thus learn something about ancient insect life by studying amber that formed at different times.

In addition to the Baltic amber, there is dark-red or orange Sicilian amber; Roumanian amber, characterized by a brownish-yellow color

Amber has been cut for centuries into beads and other ornaments (top). Coral is used for beads, cabochons, inlay work, or fine carvings (btm.), and displays various colors.

and the presence of considerable sulfur; and Chinese amber, actually primarily from Burma, dark brown to brownish-yellow in color, sometimes colorless or red, and often heavily crazed.

Reconstructed amber or pressed amber ("amberoid") is man-made, and produced by melting small bits of amber together under pressure. This material is also sometimes dyed various colors.

Amber is easily distinguished from plastic imitations by means of a needle, heated to redness. The hot needle is touched against the suspected amber, usually in an unobtrusive place, such as just inside the hole in a bead. The hot needle will burn the material, and the odor of the smoke is distinctive. Plastics give off a strong, rancid smell of camphor and carbolic acid, both of which are strong, penetrating, and unpleasant. Amber gives a pleasant, sweet smell. But other natural resins, such as copal, also give sweet odors when burned, and other tests are needed. A good test to distinguish between amber (and other natural resins) and imitations is cutting with a sharp knife. When cut, natural resins tend to chip and break into powder. Plastics and bakelite yield large chips or curled peelings.

Amber is in great demand, especially among collectors of antiques. Sicilian amber is highly prized, and transparent red or green material is the most valuable, followed by transparent yellows. Natural amber may darken with long exposure to the air, turning a mellow brown color. Pressed amber, on the other hand, may turn white as it ages. Amber is used extensively to make beads, boxes, and ornamental carved objects, and has maintained its popularity for more than 2,000 years.

Coral

Coral has been popular for thousands of years. Its curative powers were strongly believed by the ancient Romans. A piece of red coral was supposed to change color according to the state of the wearer's health. Superstition about coral was prevalent, but its magical powers would only be effective if the coral were not carved or fashioned by man. Coral held a treasured place among the inhabitants of Persia, Tibet, India, and Africa. Strings of coral were considered royal gifts in some parts of Africa, and coral was sacred in India two millennia ago.

Indians of the southwestern United States have known and prized coral for more than four centuries. Today some Indian tribes, especially the Zuni, still employ coral in their silverwork, although much of the red material used is red abalone.

Coral is the accumulated exudation of tiny marine animals. These animals, called "coral polyps," live in huge colonies and exude a deposit of calcium carbonate, the mineral calcite, to form a protective home. A coral colony always grows perpendicular to the surface of attachment. The calcium carbonate accretion formed by the polyps is **93** the material we know as coral.

There are many varieties and colors of coral. White coral is the most common; other colors include pink, orangy-pink, orange, blue, red ("precious coral"), and black ("king's coral"). Coral occurs throughout the world in warm climates and tropical waters having a temperature above 68°F. The most important sources are the Mediterranean Sea, especially along the coasts of Algeria, Morocco, Tunisia, Sardinia, and Italy. Coral usually grows in shallow water, but some varieties form at depths of 1,000 feet. The structure of coral is very distinctive: a branched, tree-like shape. Individual branches may show a fine scale striping or banding. The only common imitations are wood, wax, and celluloid, but these can usually be distinguished on the basis of hardness and microscopic examination.

Gem quality coral is uniform in color and dense enough to take a high polish. The value of any particular color is a matter of local fashion, but the deep-red variety, sometimes called "ox-blood coral," generally

commands higher prices. Pink and pale-colored coral, sometimes called "angel's-skin," can be even more expensive, and a fine, well-matched strand of beads may cost several thousand dollars. The finest coral gems come from Italy, and include beads, cameos, intaglios, figurines, carvings, and handles.

Ivory

Ivory is generally considered the material forming the tusk of an elephant, but may also include other animals, such as the hippopotamus, walrus, wart-hog, and the narwhal, an Arctic whale. Elephant ivory has a distinctive spiral structure not seen in other kinds of ivory.

94   Ivory is very dense material, and is essentially the same substance of

which teeth are composed. Its pores are filled with an oily compound that adds to the luster of its polish, and makes ivory easy to carve. Elephant tusks are actually enlarged incisor teeth, and may reach a length of 10 feet and weigh nearly 200 pounds.

Carved ivory objects have been found in tombs several thousand years old. Thrones of ancient monarchs were adorned with ivory carvings and ornaments. Fine and detailed ivory sculptures decorate museums and private collections throughout the world.

Most genuine ivory comes from Africa; exports are regulated, but a large quantity of ivory is illegally traded. Typical fabricated ivory objects include necklaces, cuff links, studs, rings, bracelets, clips, umbrella handles, piano keys, figurines, boxes, and billiard balls. Ivory is porous and easily stained. It has a tendency to turn yellow with age, a process that has been attributed to atmospheric action. Exposure to sunlight can bleach and lighten the color of ivory.

Ivory imitations include bone, horn, plastics, and plaster of Paris. In nearly all cases a simple microscopic examination will suffice to distinguish ivory from imitation materials.

Jet

Jet is a very hard variety of coal. It may have been mined in England as early as 1500 B.C., and jet beads and charms have been found in ancient burial mounds. The material was popular in Victorian times, especially worn to signify mourning for a deceased loved one.

Jet forms by the compression of lignite, a brown coal derived from buried driftwood. The classic locality is Whitby, Yorkshire, which is the locale of one of the world's oldest gem industries, specializing in the **95**

Fine cameos are carved in Italy from shells (opp. l.).
Scrimshaw (opp. r.) is artwork done on whalebone or ivory. Ivory is usually carved into useful or decorative shapes (above).

production of jet. When recovered from its host rock, Whitby jet may sometimes have the form of the original wood branches and logs. Other localities for jet include Spain, Germany, France, Nova Scotia, Colorado, and Utah.

Jet has a dull luster on broken surfaces, and a hardness of 2½–4 on the Mohs scale. It is tough and takes a good polish. Imitations include dyed chalcedony, black tourmaline, garnet, and obsidian (all are harder than jet and feel colder to the skin); bakelite (pungent odor when heated); glass (vitreous luster on broken surface); rubber, notably a hard variety called vulcanite, but this is easily distinguished because it gives a burned-rubber odor when heated. Cannel coal is a substance much like jet that occurs in the coal beds of Newcastle, England, but this is more brittle than jet.

Jet is customarily cut into beads, crosses, bracelets, cabochons, and various useful and decorative objects. The desirable attributes are pure black color with no inclusions and absence of fine cracks. Even the best jet is not expensive.

Shell

The shells of many marine animals have an iridescent luster. Most notable among these are the shells of large pearl oysters and the abalone.

Shell is used for making mother-of-pearl buttons, handles, inlay work, and ornaments. Pauna shells from New Zealand and abalone from California waters are especially colorful. Sometimes a thin slice of abalone shell is cemented to the bottom of a colorless quartz cabochon to provide an interesting opal imitation.

Cameos are carved into the Helmet shell and the Queen conch, both of which grow in the waters of the West Indies. Helmet-shell cameos are white and brown, while those from the Queen conch are white on a pink background, or vice versa.

Interesting objects, sometimes seen in jewelry, that resemble eyes are shell with circular markings. This material is called operculum.

96

Jet is a form of coal once popular in jewelry (top l.).
Shells of various kinds (top r.) are used widely in jewelry. Spodumene of
blue-green color (opp.) is rare, especially in large sizes.

Spodumene

Spodumene crystals can reach enormous size, as long as 40 feet and as heavy as 65 tons. Such crystals are never gemmy, but tend to be drab gray or pinkish objects. In fact, the name spodumene comes from a Greek word meaning "burned to ashes," in reference to the unattractive gray color. It seems hard to believe that this unlovely mineral could occur in the delicate and attractive transparent pink and green gem varieties known as kunzite and hiddenite.

The pink or lilac color variety of spodumene was named in honor of the renowned American gem expert, George F. Kunz. Emerald-green spodumene was named hiddenite after A. E. Hidden, the manager of the North Carolina mine where the crystals were first found. A third color variety is light yellow, yellow-green, or colorless, and is known simply as green spodumene or colorless spodumene.

Spodumene is a lithium aluminum silicate, hardness 7 on the Mohs scale, and is related to jade in that both minerals are members of a group of minerals known as the pyroxenes. Physically, however, jade and spodumene are vastly different, the former being tough and compact, the latter having perfect cleavage in several directions. This cleavage makes spodumene very difficult to cut and easy to break if carelessly worn. Cut spodumenes also display an asset that makes wearing them worth the risk. Spodumene is trichroic, and kunzite, for example, appears violet, deep violet, and colorless when viewed in different directions. In hiddenite the trichroic colors are bluish-green, yellow-green, and emerald-green. Spodumene is generally cut in such a way that the deepest color is seen when the viewer looks down through the table of the gem.

Spodumene has been known to mineralogists for centuries, but gem

material seems to have first come to light in Brazil in 1877. Then, in 1879 at Stony Point, North Carolina, deep-green crystals were found and named hiddenite. Fine hiddenites were never common and are now considered extremely rare and costly. Collectors will pay more than $100 per carat for a good stone, and a gem of more than two carats would be considered large.

Kunzite, on the other hand, occurs in crystals that may weigh tens of pounds. The darker the color, the more valuable the gems cut from such crystals. Top quality, deep-pink, rose, or violet-colored kunzites of large size may sell for more than $50 per carat. Cut stones weighing between 500 and 1,000 carats are exhibited in major museums. Lilac-colored spodumene was first discovered in Connecticut in 1879, and was then found in California in 1902.

The typical mode of occurrence of spodumene is in pegmatites, associated with beryl. Major occurrences of gem material are California, especially at Pala in San Diego County, the Malagasay Republic, and Burma. Madagascar spodumene shows delicate blue and green tints, along with violet, in pale-colored transparent crystals. The majority of available gem spodumene comes from Minas Gerais, Brazil. Brazilian spodumenes occur in many colors, especially pink, yellow, and yellow-green. Very rarely seen are gems with a distinctive blue-green color, known chiefly from Afghanistan.

Good hiddenite can easily be mistaken for emerald, but the extreme scarcity makes encountering such gems unlikely. In spite of its attractive color, kunzite is not familiar to most gem dealers nor to the gem-buying public. The name hiddenite should be applied only to emerald-green spodumene, and not to the more common pale-green varieties.
Consumer Tips—Synthetics are sold that strongly resemble kunzite, but many kunzites are characterized by the presence of fine tubes that can be seen under magnification or with the naked eye. Gemological tests **98** can easily distinguish kunzite from the most prevalent imitations.

Brazilian kunzite gems such as this of 23.75 carats (top l.) are widely sold, and a stone of 137 carats (top r.) is worthy of museum display. Faceted chrysoberyls, this one 12.6 carats (opp.) are seldom seen in jewelry.

Chrysoberyl

Chrysoberyl has a dominant position in the gem world, because of the rarity and high value of its varieties. These are, curiously enough, some of the least widely known gemstones, yet their names are familiar to most people.

The word "chrysoberyl" is derived from Greek words meaning "golden beryl." Yet transparent, faceted, yellow chrysoberyls are not commonly seen in jewelry and are not of great importance in the gem trade. The best-known variety of chrysoberyl is not transparent at all, but rather contains many fine, fibrous inclusions. Light reflected from these fibers is concentrated along a line when the material is cut into a cabochon, yielding an "eye." The eye in chrysoberyl is the sharpest and loveliest seen in any gem because the fibers are extremely fine and tightly packed. This is the gem known as cat's-eye chrysoberyl.

The term "cat's-eye" is commonly misused in the gem trade. The formation of a "cat's-eye" in any gemstone is a phenomenon due to the presence of fibers. The term is commonly used as an adjective, so we may have cat's-eye tourmaline, cat's-eye apatite, and so on. Throughout history, however, the term "cat's-eye" *has* been used alone in reference to a single gem: chrysoberyl.

Cat's-eye chrysoberyl is usually yellowish or greenish in color, and transparent to translucent. The most highly valued is a "honey" color, a slightly brownish-yellow hue. A distinctive feature of cat's-eye chrysoberyl is the strong "relief" of the eye—that is, the intensity with which it shines forth in the stone. Often the eye has a bluish cast.

Gem cat's-eye chrysoberyl is almost never mined *in situ,* but is nearly always recovered from stream deposits. The finest gems come from Sri Lanka and Burma, and good material is found in Minas Gerais, Brazil. The best material is ''honey-colored'' brownish-yellow, followed in value by green, dark brown, pale yellow, and greenish-yellow. The eye must be well centered and sharp, and the gem must be translucent.

The other variety of chrysoberyl of major gem significance is alexandrite. The remarkable feature of this gem is its dramatic change of color: red or violet in incandescent light to green or blue-green in sunlight. This change of color is due to the absorption of certain light wavelengths by the material. The finest alexandrite changes from a purplish red to blue-green, both colors showing a minimum brownish tint. Such spectacular stones come from the U.S.S.R., and some may ·even appear emerald-green in daylight. Stones from Sri Lanka tend to be more of an olive-green color.

Alexandrite was named after Alexander II, Czar of Russia, on whose birthday the gem was discovered. It is also interesting that red and green were the colors of the old Russian Imperial Guard.

Alexandrite is one of the most expensive gems. Large stones with a good color change can cost thousands of dollars per carat. Stones weighing more than ten carats are considered very large and might be worthy of museum display. The value of an alexandrite is a function of its size, transparency, and the quality of the color change, as well as the disposition of the marketplace.

Cat's-eye chrysoberyl has become a rare and costly gem also, with demand exceeding the supply. Fine gems weighing more than a few carats may sell for several thousand dollars per carat. Transparent faceted chrysoberyls are usually not as expensive, ranging in price from a few tens to a few hundred dollars per carat.

Transparent chrysoberyls occur in yellow, brown, green, and, very rarely, blue shades. All chrysoberyls are very hard, 8½ on the Mohs scale, so all wear well and are durable gems.

Consumer Tips—Cat's-eye chrysoberyl has not been synthesized at this time, but synthetic alexandrite is now available and shows a distinct color change of fine quality. This material is expensive to manufacture, and is therefore more costly than synthetic spinel or corundum.

A synthetic corundum containing vanadium oxide impurities has a color change vaguely reminiscent of alexandrite. The color change of this corundum is blue-gray to lilac and does not vary much from one manufacturer to another. These inexpensive gems are sold to tourists around the world as ''alexandrite.'' A sale price of a few dollars per carat should indicate that a proferred gem is not genuine alexandrite.

Peridot

An old legend says that the inhabitants of St. John's Island, also known as Zebirget, in the Red Sea off the coast of Egypt, mined green stones as early as 1500 B.C. These gems were called "topazos," and the island itself known as Topazios. The stones were greatly prized by the Egyptian kings who dominated the island, and the inhabitants were forced to mine them under rather harsh conditions. It was believed that the gems glowed in the dark, so they were hunted at night and the locations of the glowing spots carefully marked for recovery the next day. Actually, today we know topaz is a completely different gem. The material mined on Zebirget is the gem form of the mineral olivine, which we know as peridot.

Peridot is surrounded by superstition. It was once thought that it could break evil spells. The gem was associated with the sun, whose rays gave life and dispelled the mysteries of the darkness. Peridot was also supposed to have medicinal value. Through the centuries confusion arose regarding the names given to this material. The name "chrysolite" has been applied to peridot, prehnite, chrysoberyl, and other yellow stones. Other misleading names are "oriental-chrysolite" (chrysoberyl), "Brazilian-chrysolite" (also chrysoberyl), "aquamarine-chrysolite" (beryl), and "Saxony-chrysolite" (topaz). Many peridots were sent to Europe during the time of the Crusades, labeled as emeralds. Some of the finest known gems are in museums, and may attain sizes of several hundred carats.

Peridot is a warm, soft olive or yellowish-green gem. It never reaches the intensity or shade of green characteristic of emerald. The hardness is 6–7 on the Mohs scale, which is somewhat soft for a gemstone. Cut peridots therefore tend to lose their polish and become scratched after some time. Good cleavage makes peridot somewhat delicate for use in rings. The birefringence of peridot is fairly high, and back facets appear

101

*Peridot is a popular birthstone,
with gems available from Arizona (l., 7.66 carats)
and Burma (r., 5.0 carats).*

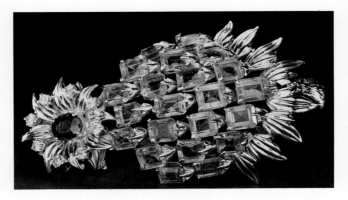

doubled when viewed through the thickness of a stone. Peridot tends to have a soft, velvety appearance that helps distinguish it from similar-appearing materials such as tourmaline and glass.

St. John's Island is still a major source of the finest peridot, although mining there is extremely sporadic. Typically, no material is mined until little or none remains available on the marketplace, thus creating renewed demand. Fine peridot of a pleasing color comes from Arizona. At this locality small pebbles of olivine have been broken out of the rocks in which the mineral formed, and are recovered from sand dunes and ant hills! The Mogok District of Burma also produces fine peridot, some of large size. Small amounts of peridot have also been found in Brazil, Australia, Czechoslovakia, Hawaii, Norway, Zaire, and Mexico.

Consumer Tips—Peridot is not an expensive gem, except in very large-sized flawless pieces. The best material is green with no tinge of brown or yellow. The finest stones may sell for several tens of dollars per carat. Gems weighing more than 50 carats are worthy of museum display.

The color range of peridot makes confusion with other stones possible. Usually color is characteristic of certain localities. This information may add enjoyment to ownership, and should be obtained at time of purchase.

Synthetic spinel the color of peridot is a widely sold birthstone substitute, but spinel has none of the diffuse, oily softness of genuine peridot, and is also much harder.

A brownish-green material resembling peridot was identified in recent years as a distinct mineral, known as sinhalite. Only the most careful tests can distinguish the two gems. Sinhalite is extremely rare and only cut stones are known, but it seems likely that many more exist that have been mislabeled peridot.

A fine pin (above) of peridot and garnet,
in yellow-gold. Crystals of lapis lazuli, or lazurite (opp.),
from Afghanistan are rare and costly.

Lapis Lazuli

Few gems display a color as rich as the deep royal blue of fine lapis. The name itself comes from an ancient Arabic word, ''allazward,'' meaning ''sky'' or ''blue.'' In ancient times lapis was known as ''sapphirus,'' although today sapphire is a name reserved for the colored varieties of corundum.

Lapis was one of the most precious commodities of the ancient world, and was even valued on an equal level with gold. Lapis was used in medicines, cosmetics, and paintings. When powdered, lapis yields an intense blue pigment known as ultramarine. The famous artist Vermeer may well have used lapis in preparing the blue paint that bears his name. Today ultramarine is manufactured synthetically.

The tomb of Tutankhamen, Pharaoh of Egypt, contained a wealth of gold and lapis jewels. The gem is known from burial sites 1,000 years older still. Lapis has been mined continuously (though sporadically) for more than 6,000 years in the Badakshan region of Afghanistan.

Lapis is actually a rock, composed chiefly of the minerals lazurite, pyrite, and calcite. Lazurite is blue, pyrite yellow, and calcite is white. The brassy-gold spots and flecks of pyrite in genuine lapis are very distinctive. The hardness of lapis (specifically the lazurite component) is

5½–6 on the Mohs scale. Lapis is usually made into cabochons or polished flat wafers, carved or made into boxes and beads. In spite of the relatively low hardness, scratches can easily be polished out, so the gem wears well.

Fine lapis often has a violet cast. Material resembling that from Afghanistan has been found in the U.S.S.R. This has pyrite spots and occurs in various shades of blue. The Russian royalty used lapis extensively in construction, and some rooms built by Catherine II, for example, are lined with slabs of fine lapis.

Lapis also occurs in quantity in the Andes Mountains of Chile. This material is paler in color than Siberian or Afghan lapis, is heavily veined or spotted with white or grayish calcite, and sometimes has a greenish coloration. This is the least valuable type of lapis. Small quantities of lapis have been found in southern California, Labrador, Burma, Angola, and Pakistan.

So-called "Persian lapis" actually comes from Afghanistan. "Swiss lapis" and "German lapis" are both blue-dyed chalcedony. Glass is commonly used to imitate lapis, but the fracture surface of glass is bright, whereas genuine lapis breaks with a dull, uneven fracture. A sintered synthetic spinel colored by cobalt is an effective imitation, and actually contains flakes of genuine gold to imitate pyrite inclusions. Some lapis is dyed to enhance its color. Pierre Gilson of Paris has produced synthetic lapis, containing pyrite flakes, that is visually identical to fine Afghan lapis.

The finest natural gem material is a dark-blue color with a violet cast, uniformly colored and displaying no white spots. The best material may sell for more than $10 per carat. Carvings made of large solid blocks are very costly. A wide variety of carved objects has been made from lapis. Cabochons are used primarily in men's jewelry, for which lapis is eminently suited because of its rich color and durability.

Consumer Tips—Imitation lapis may be very realistic and careful examination may be required to identify it. Fine lapis is plentiful enough to satisfy existing demand and keep prices at a fairly low level. Fine "Persian" (Afghanistan) lapis often has small white spots on a blue background. Stones cut from such material are frequently "touched up" with dye to color in these white areas, even though the entire stone might not be dyed and the color of the lapis itself is natural in origin. It is always wise to inquire at the time of purchase whether lapis has been treated in any way, and have this indicated on the sales slip. The presence of pyrite is a good indication of genuine lapis.

However, a new synthetic lapis manufactured by Pierre Gilson of Paris contains actual inclusions of pyrite. This may pose detection problems in the future.

104

Turquoise occurs throughout the southwestern United States. Large nuggets of fine color (opp.), however, are rare and may be very costly.

Turquoise

Turquoise, prized since remotest antiquity for its superb blue color, was known to the women of ancient Egypt. Pieces of turquoise jewelry found on a mummy dated at 7,500 years old may well be the oldest wrought jewelry items known. The mountains of the Sinai yielded this ancient treasure to the miners of the Pharaohs centuries before the Exodus of Israel. Turquoise was prized by many ancient cultures, including those of Egypt, Persia, Tibet, and the Aztecs and Incas of Central America. Turquoise was used as money by American Indians of the 16th Century, and the gem is associated with religious rites of the Navajos and other tribes. The importance of turquoise to the American Indian continues to the present day.

Native turquoise occurs primarily as crusts, nodules, veins, and seams deposited by groundwaters. The mineral is a hydrous copper aluminum phosphate; the rich blue colors are ascribed to copper, while the presence of iron introduces a greenish cast. Some of the world's finest turquoise comes from northeastern Iran (Persia). This source supplied a large portion of the turquoise imported by Europe and Asia for centuries, and turquoise was a major Iranian export before World War I. The oldest turquoise mines known are in the Sinai Desert at a place called Maghara Wadi. Minor amounts of turquoise are found in China, Australia, Tibet, Peru, Mexico, Chile, and Afghanistan.

Today the United States is a major world source of turquoise. Most of the mines are in Arizona and New Mexico, with some production from

Colorado, Nevada, and California. Mining is simple, because turquoise is usually deposited at or near the surface, and only shallow pits or trenches are needed. Most mining is done by hand.

There are several basic grades of turquoise. Turquoise matrix is material in which blue or green gem material is mixed with portions of brownish or gray rock. Sometimes the matrix is in the form of an intricate lace-like pattern, known as spiderweb. So-called Egyptian turquoise is yellowish-green or greenish-blue. American turquoise is found in all shades of blue and green, usually with some matrix present. Persian turquoise is dense and non-porous, so it takes a high polish. This is among the finest turquoise, and is characterized by a uniform and intense pale-blue or medium-blue color.

The best quality turquoise is uniform in color, deep blue, and free of matrix. Such stones may sell for tens of dollars per carat. Just below this in value is fine quality spiderweb turquoise; value decreases with increasing amounts of matrix. In all cases valuation is based on overall appearance and depth of color, as well as the presence or absence of green or brown tinge. Uniformity of color implies the absence of off-color patches or spots. Dark-blue turquoise is considered the most desirable, while greenish-blue stones are of lesser quality. Yellowish-green material may sell for a few pennies per carat.

Turquoise is somewhat soft—6 on the Mohs scale—but is compact and wears well. Turquoise is always opaque, and therefore is cut into beads and cabochons that sometimes take a high polish and have a glassy appearance. Small chips are extensively used by Indian workers and silversmiths for inlay purposes, and Indian jewelry with turquoise set in silver has become very popular. The variety of rings, bracelets, pendants, and earrings produced is enormous. Of special interest and popularity are the ornate necklaces called "squashblossom" that can weigh several pounds and may cost thousands of dollars, depending on the quality of turquoise they contain and the intricacy of the workmanship. American turquoise, with its deep-blue shades, is well qualified for this kind of work, because light-colored Persian turquoise loses effec-

tiveness when set in brightly polished silver. Most Indian craftsmen prefer to cut baroque, or free-form cabochons, rather than standard-sized ovals and other geometric shapes. Persian turquoise, on the other hand, is routinely cut to standard shapes and sizes.

Some turquoise is carved into animal figures and other decorative shapes. Turquoise beads are usually baroque shapes or tumble-polished nuggets. Occasionally a gem buyer will find a strand of matched round beads, perhaps of spiderweb material. Such a necklace may sell for several thousand dollars if the quality of the turquoise is high.

The porosity of turquoise allows the material to absorb various additives designed to improve the color. These additives include oils, wax, and plastics. Soaking in a solvent such as carbon tetrachloride is a good way of detecting such treatment, but also drastically affects the appearance of the turquoise when the additive is dissolved out. Sometimes an oiled or "waxed" turquoise gem will "sweat" if heated or placed in the sun. Stones treated with plastics or sodium silicate (water glass) are harder to detect. Unfortunately much of the turquoise sold has been treated in some way.

Consumer Tips—In buying turquoise the consumer might wish to obtain a guarantee that the color will be maintained for a specific period of time, or that the material has been checked for treatment and what the treatment was. This is especially important in the case of expensive jewelry containing turquoise represented as "natural color." All turquoise offered for sale should be viewed with the thought of possible prior treatment.

Turquoise has been synthetically produced by Pierre Gilson of Paris. This synthetic is dense, uniform in color, and takes a high polish. It resembles the very finest Persian turquoise, but is priced much lower. **107**

Turquoise colors include various shades of blue and green (opp. l.),
while Persian turquoise is generally a fine blue of uniform color (opp. r.). American
Indian jewelry of turquoise and silver (above) is very popular.

Decorative Stones

Malachite and Azurite

Malachite is an important copper ore that also makes an attractive gemstone. It has been known and used in jewelry since the days of ancient Egypt, as early as 4000 B.C. For millennia it was considered a magical stone with potent powers. Crystals are rare and highly esteemed among mineral collectors. Massive banded material is much more abundant, notably from Zaire. Other localities for malachite include France, England, Rhodesia, New Mexico, and Arizona. In many localities malachite, which is always some shade of green, is mixed with blue azurite. Both minerals are copper carbonates. Their association is widespread, and azurite is frequently found altering to malachite. Azurite is seldom used for gem purposes, and massive deposits of it, comparable to those of malachite, do not exist.

Malachite is soft, only 3½–4 on the Mohs scale; the same is true of azurite. Both minerals take a high polish, but the polish is lost relatively quickly with wear, due to scratching. Massive banded material is dense and compact, but is not very tough and should always be set and worn with great care.

Malachite is customarily made into beads, cabochons, and a variety of carved shapes, such as figurines and ashtrays. Large deposits of very fine banded malachite in the U.S.S.R. found use in buildings, and whole rooms in certain palaces were lined with malachite slabs. Russian workmanship in this gem is unsurpassed.

Malachite from Clifton, Arizona (above) displays banding and "bull's-eye" patterns. Variscite from Lewiston, Utah (opp.) is characteristically mixed with other phosphate minerals in nodules.

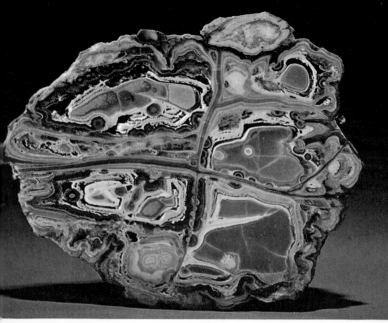

Chrysocolla

Chrysocolla is a hydrated copper silicate. It forms as an alteration product in copper deposits, in veins and cracks, or as a coating on rocks. Sometimes it accumulates in sufficient thickness to be cut into gemstones. More frequently chrysocolla merely stains chalcedony, producing an intense blue material that is also tough and durable. The color of chrysocolla depends on its purity, and ranges from pale blue to dark blue, blue-green, and yellow-green. The finest material is translucent, uniform blue in color, and free of off-color spots. The hardness of chrysocolla is only 2–4 on the Mohs scale, but the material frequently contains enough silica to become hard, and it will then take a high polish. Localities for chrysocolla include Nevada, New Mexico, Arizona, Chile, and the U.S.S.R.

Variscite

Variscite is an aluminum phosphate with a lovely yellow-green to blue-green color. It commonly forms nodules associated with other phosphate minerals, in intricate banded and patterned textures. The hardness is only 4–5 on the Mohs scale, and the material is neither tough nor durable. The only important localities are in Utah, where the nodules can reach diameters up to 1 foot. The usual form of cutting is cabochons and polished slabs. Some tradenames applied to variscite in **109**

the past include "amatrix," for American matrix, "Nevada turquoise," "California turquoise," and "Utahlite." Amatrix is a mixture of variscite in quartz or chalcedony, and so somewhat harder than pure variscite.

Sodalite

Sodalite is an attractive, deep-smalt-blue mineral, chemically composed of sodium aluminum silicate. Crystals are extremely rare, but massive material is abundant in certain localities. Sodalite is one of the mineral components of the rock lapis lazuli, but became an important ornamental material in its own right when large deposits were found in Ontario, Canada.

The hardness of sodalite is 5½–6 on the Mohs scale, which is adequate for the cabochons and beads usually fashioned from the material. Slabs are also polished and used in inlaid boxes and clocks. Canada is the most important source, but other localities include Norway, India, Maine, and Massachusetts. A beautiful, almost transparent blue sodalite comes from South West Africa.

Sodalite is quite inexpensive, and hobbyists can obtain rough material at a cost of several dollars per pound. Large blocks of sodalite are **110** frequently cut into animal figures and other decorative shapes.

Russian malachite (top l.) makes fine cabochons, as does sodalite (top r.). Chrysocolla (btm. l.) is durable and richly colored. Rhodonite (btm. r.) is used widely as a decorative stone.

Rhodonite

Rhodonite is manganese silicate. Crystals are not rare, but found in only a few localities. Transparent material from such crystals is occasionally faceted for collectors. But of far greater significance to the gem trade is massive rhodonite. This is available in large quantities, in colors ranging from rose-red and pink to brownish-pink. Often the pink material is heavily mottled with dense black patterns of manganese oxide, producing a very attractive decorative stone.

Rhodonite occurs in Australia, Sweden, and the U.S.S.R. in commercial quantities. Translucent material is commonly made into cabochons and beads, while more opaque rhodonite is used for inlay work and carving. Fine translucent beads can be costly, but cabochons routinely sell for a few dollars.

Gem carvers use rhodonite extensively because of its toughness and interesting patterns. Hinged boxes, made primarily in Germany, may feature thin rhodonite slabs overlaying white marble.

Spinel

Set prominently in the front of the Imperial State Crown of England is a huge red gem that flashes a fiery brilliance. This stone is known throughout the world as the Black Prince's Ruby. First recorded historically in 1367, the gem has followed a long and romantic series of adventures, ultimately ending its travels in the British Crown Jewels. The stone is enormous—2 inches across—and is simply a polished, rough mass. Unfortunately, it is not a ruby, as was so long thought. Rather, it is one of the world's finest examples of red spinel, sometimes called "ballas ruby."

Spinel is a fascinating gem that occurs in a wide range of colors, including carmine-red, blood-red (so-called "ruby spinel"), brownish-red, rose-red, orange, pale blue, violet-blue, dark blue, purple, greenish, and black. Star spinels are known but are extremely rare. Spinel is a magnesium aluminum oxide, but chemical substitution

Spinel of
fine red color may
resemble ruby.

111

produces a variety of other mineral species that share the same general atomic structure. Pure spinel is actually colorless; the wide variety of existing colors is due to the presence of impurities.

Large fine spinels are great treasures, yet few people know of their existence. This is largely because spinel occurs associated with ruby and sapphire. For centuries therefore, spinel has existed in the shadow of its more prominent and valuable cousins. The colors of gem spinels are intense and vibrant. The hardness of 8 on the Mohs scale makes spinel one of the harder and more durable gems. Yet the price is kept low by lack of demand. Ruby spinel is the most highly prized, yet will seldom reach several hundred dollars per carat in price. A ruby of identical appearance would sell for thousands of dollars per carat.

Spinels tend to have fewer flaws than corundum gems of comparable color, size, and quality. However, large rough spinels are quite rare and might be fit for museum display. The Diamond Treasury in Moscow contains a huge deep-red spinel, clear, transparent, and irregular in shape. It is set at the top of a crown made for the Princess Catherine II in 1762. The stone weighs an estimated 400 carats. A gem of 105 carats is in the collection of the Louvre in Paris, and the British Museum of Natural History, London, displays a polished mass from Burma that weighs 520 carats. Cut spinels weighing more than ten carats can be considered rare gems. Although they are available, few cut spinels are sold because of the almost complete unfamiliarity with spinel on the part of the general public.

The world's most notable localities for gem spinel are the gem gravels of Sri Lanka and Burma. The gem rough may occur as perfect crystals, waterworn pebbles, or large irregular lumps. Other localities include Afghanistan, Thailand, Australia, Brazil, and the United States. Many historically important stones came from the ruby mines of Badakshan, Afghanistan.

Synthetic spinels have been manufactured since about 1915. The colors produced are generally designed to mimic the appearance of other gemstones, such as aquamarine and tourmaline, rather than the natural colors of spinel or corundum! Synthetic spinels are commonly seen in class rings and inexpensive birthstone jewelry, usually labeled (erroneously) in quotes, such as ''tourmaline'' or ''topaz.''

Consumer Tips—A buyer's suspicions must surely be aroused when a ''topaz'' in a 14K gold ring is priced at $40 or less, since a precious topaz of the same size and color might easily sell for ten times that amount.

Spinels occur in such a wide variety of natural colors that they could easily be mistaken for other gems. Since they are very hard, lovely, and durable, spinels should be more popular than they are; their current neglect is due to a lack of exposure to the public by the jewelry trade.

Zircon occurs in a wide range of colors, but most stones seen in jewelry (opp.) are blue and colorless gems, both colors produced by heat treatment.

Zircon

Records of the first uses of zircon as a gemstone are hidden in the dark shrouds of a forgotten past. Carved zircons have been recovered from some of the most ancient of dated archaeological sites, and zircon may have been the earliest used of all gems. It appears in the Bible and it recurs through world literature under a variety of names, including jacinth, hyacinth, and jargoon. Zircon was respected in the Middle Ages for its supposed curative powers.

There are three distinct types of zircon, generally known as high, medium, and low. The chemical composition is basically zirconium silicate, but the presence of radioactive elements in the structure and its complex mode of formation makes zircon one of the more interesting gem minerals. In addition, zirconium metal is extensively used in space-age alloys with sophisticated applications. Non-gem zircon is therefore mined in large quantities for its zirconium content.

For gem purposes high-type zircon is the most important. The primary sources are Cambodia and Thailand, where it is found as waterworn pebbles colored reddish-brown to yellowish-brown. The pebbles are heated in primitive coal-burning ovens, sometimes several times. The treatment causes a color change, producing blue, golden-yellow, and colorless material. Bangkok is a cutting and heating center for zircon. Occasionally red or orange stones appear on the market, but these

colors are natural in origin and not produced by heating.

Low-type zircon of gem quality is found in Sri Lanka, as worn pebbles in the gem gravels. Low-zircon natural colors are yellow-green, grayish, orange, and brown; these colors are not improved by heating. Often such stones are mixed into parcels of other gems, such as sapphires or tourmalines, where their true identity is disguised.

Medium-type zircon is also found in Sri Lanka. Sometimes heating produces properties like the high type, but more often heating is unsuccessful at improving the yellow and brownish natural colors. The presence of radioactive elements in zircon ultimately causes destruction of the crystalline structure. This process is called metamictization.

Zircon itself is not a rare mineral, and occurs throughout the world. Crystals are common in various types of rocks. In addition to Sri Lanka, Cambodia, and Thailand, sources of gem material include New South Wales, Australia, and the Malagasay Republic.

Some colorless zircons of natural occurrence exist, but most blue and colorless stones are the result of heat treatment. The hardness of zircon is 6½–7 on the Mohs scale. Although there is no distinct cleavage, zircon is very brittle and should be handled and worn with care. Optically, zircon is distinctive, because it is one of the few natural gems with dispersion that approaches that of diamond. In addition, the refractive index of zircon is very high. Colorless zircons cut as round brilliants therefore have much of the steely brilliance and dispersive color play of diamond. These stones can easily be mistaken for diamonds at first glance. However, diamond is singly refractive, whereas zircon has such intense double refraction that back facets of a cut stone may appear doubled when viewed through the table. This test alone may be diagnostic, if the doubling is apparent. Sometimes the zircon is oriented in a direction for cutting that eliminates the doubling. In such cases gemological tests may be necessary.

Consumer Tips—The brittleness of zircon makes it especially susceptible to damage when worn in a ring. Stones in a parcel that are allowed to roll against each other may actually show slight damage due to chipping of facet edges. For this reason cut zircons are individually wrapped in paper for shipment.

Colorless and blue zircons, the most familiar and popular color varieties, are not very expensive and can usually be purchased for a few dollars per carat. Very large stones, however, are rare.

Small zircons may be used as side stones in jewelry, in place of diamond chips. Examination with a strong hand lens or microscope will readily reveal such substitution, since the zircons will show facet doubling and signs of wear, whereas diamonds would retain their polish and show less chipping.

114

Tanzanite from Tanzania (opp.), once virtually unknown in the gem trade, has become a rare, popular, and costly gem. The cutting on the stones pictured is unusually fine.

Tanzanite

Prior to 1967 the only variety of the mineral zoisite used for gems was a pink-colored, massive material known as thulite. In 1967 transparent crystals of violet-blue zoisite were found in Tanga Province, Tanzania, and later in various deposits in the Umba valley.

The crystals occur in various colors, including brown, pink, yellow, blue, and green; many crystals are strongly trichroic. Careful heating at about 700° F, however, turns most of these crystals a uniform, deep violet-blue color. Exquisite gems have been cut from this material, to which Tiffany & Co. gave the tradename tanzanite. Initially a large quantity of material was available, and prices of even large stones varied up to a few tens of dollars per carat. By 1975 the retail price of large gems, weighing more than ten carats, could be measured in hundreds of dollars per carat. Tanzanite offers a striking testimony to the rapid and sizable appreciation possible in certain gems.

The hardness of tanzanite on the Mohs scale is only 6, so the gem is a poor choice for a ringstone. In addition there is one direction of perfect cleavage that makes wear in a ring inadvisable. The best tanzanites, however, resemble fine blue sapphires, and it is easy to see why they have become so popular.

Tanzanite is known only from Tanzania, and decreasing production at the mines has made fine gems scarce. Stones under two carats are available in fair quantity, but larger stones that have no internal flaws or inclusions are rare and costly.

Collectors' Gems

Rhodochrosite crystals from South Africa are richly colored and prized by collectors. Occasionally such crystals provide facetable material.

Collectors' Gems

There are many minerals that sometimes occur in transparent crystals and can be faceted, or have pleasing colors and patterns that make handsome cabochons. Unfortunately, the quantity of such material is insufficient to allow widespread commercialization, and these gems are therefore considered collector stones.

The collector market is lively and growing rapidly. Rare stones can be seen in large museums, but most are in private collections. Very few dealers handle them (see page 156) and they are almost never seen in shops. Many are spectacularly beautiful, with colors not available in the better-known gem varieties. Many are far too soft and fragile to be used in jewelry. But the world of gemstones is greatly enriched by their presence, and a passing knowledge of rare stones adds spice and enjoyment to a general appreciation of gems.

The following descriptions are intended only for reference, and to indicate gem species occasionally seen or discussed by collectors and connoisseurs of gems. Some are encountered in the gem trade masquerading as other stones. Many other gem species are known, but space limitations prevent inclusion here.

Amblygonite: A rare phosphate mineral, generally colored yellow; also brown, blue, green, and pink, sometimes colorless. Hardness 6, conchoidal fracture, and one good cleavage direction. Localities include Brazil, California, South Dakota, Maine, Spain, and Norway. Cut gems may resemble spodumene. Stones over 20 carats available.

Andalusite: Available in sufficient quantity to be popularized on a limited scale, and may be seen in jewelry. Most frequently cut in stones of one–two carats, larger gems are rare. Named after Andalusia, Spain, where first found; occurs sparingly in the gem gravels of Sri Lanka but most gem material is from Brazil. Andalusite is very dichroic, the colors being brownish-green and reddish-brown; rarely seen are brown, pink, and violet stones. Hardness is 7½, cleavage distinct, but the material is tough and wears well. Stones are generally cut so that two of the pleochroic colors are both visible at the same time, usually green in the center and brown at the ends. Cut andalusites may resemble tourmaline. Opaque material sometimes contains a black, cross-like core and is known as chiastolite. Localities for chiastolite include Maine, Massachusetts, and the U.S.S.R.

Apatite: This would be a fine gem if not so soft, only 5 on the Mohs scale. The color range includes yellow, violet, blue, green, brown, and white. Apatite is calcium phosphate, with no distinct cleavage and uneven fracture. Faceted gems are relatively easy to cut and take a high polish. Sometimes fibrous inclusions will produce a cat's-eye effect. Gem material comes from Mexico (yellow), Sri Lanka (blue), Norway (blue-green), Canada (green, brown), India (green), Germany (violet), and Maine (violet). Apatite has been synthesized for use in lasers, but cut synthetics are not sold commercially.

Apatite is the material of which bones and teeth are made. Organically created crystals tend to be extremely small, whereas mineral crystals may reach a length of several feet!

119

Andalusite (opp. top) is beautiful and inexpensive.
Amblygonite (opp. btm.) is available in large sizes, and apatite (above) provides a huge color palette for the gem collector.

Benitoite: One of the rarest and most beautiful gems, it was first discovered in 1906. The only significant locality is in southern California. Gems may be colorless and pink, but most commonly are sapphire-blue. The dispersion of benitoite is equal to that of diamond, and stones cut to diamond angles and proportions may look like blue diamonds. The hardness is about 6–6½ and tenacity is poor, but the beautiful color and dispersion make benitoite a most desirable gem. Unfortunately, very little material exists, and cut stones over one carat are considered large and rare. Most existing cut benitoites are round brilliant gems. The largest cut stones weigh less than 15 carats.

Brazilianite: This phosphate mineral was first discovered in Brazil in 1944, happily in large, beautiful crystals that somewhat resemble chrysoberyl in color. The hardness is only 5½ and the cleavage is excellent, so cut brazilianites are too delicate to wear. But the strong yellow color is attractive and large rough is available. Gem material comes only from Brazil, and cut gems can easily be distinguished from **120** similar-appearing stones by standard gemological tests.

Calcite: One of the most common minerals on earth, calcite is calcium carbonate and makes up the rocks known as limestone and marble. In massive form, as marbles, attractive banded material is cut for ornamental uses and building facings, as well as tabletops and carvings. Calcite crystals occur in a wide range of colors and sometimes in large, transparent crystals. The hardness is only 3 and cleavage is excellent in three directions, so gems are delicate and very difficult to facet. Few stones are available even for collectors, because the cost of material is too low to make the faceting effort seem worthwhile. Yet the price per carat may be high because of cutting problems.

Cuprite: Cuprite is copper oxide, and until 1974 was not really well known as a gem material. Then a single pocket of large, transparent crystals was found in South West Africa, some of which can yield flawless gems weighing more than 100 carats. The hardness is only $3\frac{1}{2}$–4, but the rich blood-red color is spectacular. Collectors have snapped up these stones almost as quickly as they are cut, for the available supply is very limited.

Benitoite (opp. top) is found only in California. Calcite (opp. btm.) containing cobalt is pink while material from Baja California is yellow. Cuprite (top) is rare, while brazilianite (btm.) is not difficult to obtain.

121

Chrome diopside (below) and diopside (r.) are not found in jewelry, whereas star enstatite (btm.) is commercially available at low cost.

Diopside: Diopside is a very common mineral with worldwide occurrence, and is related to jadeite. The color is usually green, but may be pale to dark in shade. The hardness is only 5–6 and the easy cleavage prevents its widespread use as a faceted gem. Color varieties with special names include malacolite (pale green), alaite (colorless), and violane (massive violet). Gem crystals come from Austria, Italy, New York, Ontario, and Switzerland. Burma and India produce massive dark-green or black material that has metallic-looking inclusions. Cabochons cut from this material display cat's-eyes or four-rayed stars. Both faceted and cabochon varieties are inexpensive.

Enstatite: Related to diopside, spodumene, and jadeite, enstatite rarely occurs in transparent crystals from which brown or green gems can be cut. These are usually very dark, with a hardness of 5½ on the Mohs scale. Attractive green enstatites suffer from easy cleavage and poor toughness and are therefore collector stones, but low in price. Star enstatites are fairly common. Localities include South Africa, Burma, and India.

Euclase: An attractive gem material, euclase could be an important gem if not for its scarcity and perfect cleavage. The color range is colorless to pale blue, yellowish-green, pale yellow, and violet. Blue stones are the most popular, and the hardness of 7½ allows them to be worn. Gems weighing more than two to three carats are rare and can be expensive. Major localities include Brazil and Tanzania.

Fluorite: This common mineral occurs throughout the world in fine crystals, many of which are large and transparent. Colors include white, yellow, brown, green, violet, and blue, but the hardness is only 4 and fluorite cleaves readily. Faceted gems cannot be worn without risk, but massive fluorite, sometimes called "blue john," has been widely used for carvings and ornamental purposes. The refractive index of 1.43 is nearly the lowest of any gem material, but attractive stones can still be cut, sometimes of more than 100 carats. Green fluorite sometimes passes in carved form for pale emerald, but the hardness eventually reveals its identity.

123

Euclase (above l.) can be expensive in large sizes. Chrome fluorite (r.) from Africa is colorful but fragile.

Idocrase: Sometimes called vesuvianite, this mineral occurs in fine crystals throughout the world. A massive green or yellow-green variety that closely resembles jade is known as californite. Faceted gems are bright and beautiful, though rare, and the color range is enormous: colorless, pale yellow, yellow-green, green, brownish-green, pale blue, violet, and brown. The hardness is 6½, with indistinct cleavage and good toughness. Gemmy material comes from Canada, Italy, Pakistan, Switzerland, and Africa.

Iolite: Iolite is the gem name of the mineral cordierite, which is a silicate of aluminum and magnesium. The hardness is 7–7½, with fair toughness due to a good cleavage. Iolite is easily recognized by its intense trichroism: colorless, light blue, and sapphire-blue, and that blue color has led to the misnomer "water sapphire." Gems are usually cut so only the blue color is seen, but a stone viewed from the side will appear gray. Inclusions of an iron mineral sometimes give stones from Sri Lanka a reddish color. Localities include India, Brazil, Burma, Norway, Finland, and the Malagasay Republic. Iolite is inexpensive and often turns up in a parcel of sapphires.

Kornerupine: This is an extremely rare gem sought by collectors, usually appearing in shades of green and brown. A variety rich in chromium has a pleasing apple-green color, and yellowish stones from Canada are known. Some cat's-eyes are also known. The hardness is 6½ and most gems come from Sri Lanka, Burma, and the Malagasay Republic.

Manganotantalite: This very rare gem material is soft (6–6½) and cleaves easily, so cut gems are highly prized by collectors and can be expensive. The color is dark brownish-red.

Proustite: More important to mineral collectors for its fine crystals, proustite is a silver arsenic sulfide that occurs in a striking blood-red or crimson color. Cut gems are very rare but very lovely. The hardness is low, 2½ on the Mohs scale, so faceted gems are suitable only for collections.

*Manganotantalite
(opp.) is very rare, as
is proustite (top)
from Germany.
Iolite (above)
is commercially available
at modest cost.
Idocrase from Africa (l.)
and other localities
is hard to find,
and kornerupine
(below) is considered
a rare gem.*

Rhodochrosite: A manganese carbonate mineral, rhodochrosite is rare in facetable crystals. The hardness is low (3–4) and cleavage is excellent in three directions, because rhodochrosite is very similar in structure to calcite. But the striking pink or rose-red color provides extremely beautiful faceted gems. Such stones are usually under ten carats in weight.

Massive banded rhodochrosite occurs in quantity in Argentina, where it makes up a substantial portion of a carbonate cave. The stalactites and stalagmites in this cave are pink and white rhodochrosite, rather than the more commonly seen calcite. Cabochons of patterned rhodochrosite are popular among gem hobbyists, and rough material is available in quantity.

Scapolite: Little known to the gem trade but very beautiful when cut, scapolite occurs in fine transparent crystals in colors including colorless, yellow, pink, green, and violet-blue. The hardness is 5½–6 with perfect cleavage present, so cut gems are delicate. Fibrous inclusions in scapolite produce a fine cat's-eye effect, or a chatoyancy similar to that of moonstone. Principal localities are Burma, the Malagasay Republic,

Brazil, Siberia, and Canada.

Scapolite (above) and cat's-eye scapolite (top r.) are collectors' gems. Scheelite (top l.) makes spectacular gems.

Scheelite: Scheelite is calcium tungstate, an important ore of tungsten. Crystals are, in general, rare, and facetable crystals rarer still. The hardness is 4½–5 on the Mohs scale, with no pronounced cleavage. The stone is cut only for collectors, and may occur in colorless, pale-yellow, brownish, or orange crystals. Good gem material comes from California, Arizona, and Mexico.

Serpentine: Few materials are as readily confused with jade as serpentine, especially the variety called bowenite. Serpentine colors are much like those of jade, in the green and yellowish range. Mottled dark-green bowenite is called "verd antique" and is used as a building stone. Bowenite is softer than jade and has a lower S.G. and refractive index. The hardness of serpentine is 2½–4, that of bowenite 5–5½. Both materials are extensively used for carving and cabochons. There is tremendous variety in the texture, color, and appearance of serpentine minerals, and confusion is commonplace. Detailed gemological tests are usually required to verify the authenticity of a jade item, but the simplest preliminary test is simply to scratch the item in question!

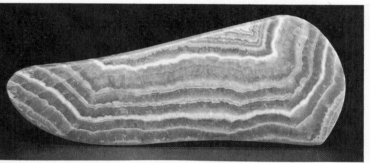

Rhodochrosite (btm.) is rarely faceted.
Massive rhodochrosite from Argentina (top), however,
is widely cut by hobbyists.

Sphalerite is rare in sizes such as this 78.4-carat giant (top). Sphene (btm.) is colorful and durable. Thomsonite (opp. top) is not well known to the public. Wulfenite (opp. btm.) is very rare when faceted, although crystals are common.

Sphalerite: Sphalerite is zinc sulfide, the world's principal orè of zinc. It is mined in enormous tonnages throughout the world, but crystals are usually black or opaque red-orange. Sometimes transparent masses are found, typically red-orange in color, sometimes yellow or greenish. The hardness is only 3½ and the perfect cleavage in six directions makes cutting and wearing difficult, but the dispersion is nearly four times that of diamond. Properly faceted gems are truly dazzling and colorful. Facetable material comes from Spain, Colorado, and Japan.

Sphene: Sometimes known as titanite, sphene is seen often enough in jewelry to be classified as an almost commercial stone. The color may be green, brown, yellow, or some combination of these three, and a chrome-green colored sphene also exists, but is extremely rare. The hardness is 5–5½ and toughness only fair; sphene tends to be brittle. But the dispersion is slightly higher than that of diamond, so faceted gems are fiery and brilliant. The usual cutting style is the round brilliant. Gem material comes from Brazil and Baja California. Fine cut stones may sell for more than $100 per carat.

Thomsonite: A complex silicate mineral, thomsonite is usually found as opaque banded material in shades of brown, green, yellow, pink, and white. The only noteworthy locality is Harbor Bay, Lake Superior. The hardness is 5–5½, with good toughness. Thomsonite usually forms as cavity fillings in volcanic rock. Weathering of the rock releases the thomsonite which is tumbled into rounded pebbles.

Wulfenite: A rare and beautiful gem, wulfenite is lead molybdate, an ore of molybdenum and lead. Its crystals, occurring in shades of yellow, orange, and red, are highly prized by mineral collectors. Cut gems have high dispersion and are spectacularly colorful. Of equal value to gem collectors are stones displaying a rich orange or deep-red color. The mineral is soft, only 3 on the Mohs scale, very brittle, and difficult to cut. Pale-yellow crystals from Tsumeb, South West Africa have afforded gems weighing more than ten carats. These resemble off-color diamonds. Localities for gem material are limited: Arizona and South West Africa.

Man-Made Gems

*Synthetic rutile was
the first popular
diamond imitation material
to come from modern laboratories.
Its dispersion is so high
that it doesn't really make
an effective substitute.*

Man-Made Gems

The creation of gems in the laboratory has been a goal of scientists and entrepreneurs for many years. Today most of the popular gemstones can be synthesized, that is, manufactured in a laboratory or factory from chemical raw materials.

It is important to distinguish between synthetics and imitations. An imitation is a material that has some of the desirable characteristics of a more costly material. A synthetic is a man-made duplication of a naturally occurring substance.

One of the oldest imitation-substitutes is glass. Glass has been manufactured for thousands of years. Glassmaking was considered a great art by the ancient Egyptians, and Greek and Roman jewelry studded with glass replicas of gems can be seen in museums. Even today glass is a widely used and popular substitute for colored gems such as ruby, emerald, and amethyst, and it can sometimes be effective and attractive. Frequently glass stones are set with a backing of metallic foil. The foil reflects light and creates a far greater brilliance than the glass alone could achieve. But glass lacks the hardness and dispersion of many natural gemstones, and man has long sought better gem substitutes.

One by one, during the past hundred years, each of the major gems has been manufactured in the laboratory. The first to appear were ruby and sapphire, followed by spinel, emerald, diamond, opal, turquoise, and chrysoberyl. These synthetic gems are optically and chemically identical with their natural counterparts. For example, natural ruby is aluminum oxide, colored red by chromium, that crystallizes in forms with hexagonal symmetry. Synthetic ruby is usually made by melting aluminum oxide that contains a trace of chromium. The resulting crystal has the same internal atomic structure as natural ruby, as well as the same optical properties, hardness, and chemical composition. In fact, the only significant difference between this material and natural ruby is the place of origin: a laboratory rather than deep within the earth. Fortunately for the gem trade, there are ways to distinguish between natural and synthetic gems. These are based chiefly on tell-tale internal markings. In natural gems there are frequently distinctive inclusions, either gas bubbles, liquid inclusions, or crystals of other minerals. In synthetics we find round bubbles, curved growth lines, and various other markings that reveal the manufactured origin.

In recent years technological developments in the areas of semiconductors and lasers have required the development of new and special crystals with useful optical or electronic properties. Some of these are brightly colored or have other characteristics suitable for gem

use. These new synthetic gems have no natural counterparts. They are unique laboratory creations that have extended the world of gemstones in new and unique directions.

It is important to remember that even imitation materials are sometimes so good at mimicking natural gems that the eye alone cannot tell the difference. A safe generalization is that, with few exceptions, *the authenticity of a gem cannot be determined with the naked eye.* Color is not a suitable criterion, because nearly any color can be duplicated with the right combination of chemicals. Synthetics can be manufactured that so resemble natural gems even gemologists are sometimes fooled. Manufacturers may try to purposely add inclusions to their products that resemble natural inclusions. Gem synthesis has become a major business, and manufacturing techniques have become a fine art. Detection **133**

A wide variety of synthetic materials, such as sapphire and ruby, is manufactured and fabricated into useful shapes as well as cut into gemstones.

of synthetics is currently a major problem, and should be entrusted only to a professional gemologist or gem laboratory, such as those of the Gemological Institute of America in New York and Los Angeles. The jeweler who might "authenticate" a stone by squinting at it against a sunlit window is often fooling both himself and his client.

There is nothing inherently wrong with synthetic gems. They bring the colors and brilliance of the finest gems within the financial means of a vast portion of the gem-loving populace. The markets for synthetic and natural gems are separate and distinct, and problems arise only when a synthetic is sold as a natural stone. For example, a five-carat ruby of the finest color and transparency might cost $10,000 per carat or more. A synthetic ruby of identical color and clarity that would, to the eye, be indistinguishable from the natural stone might sell for $20 or less. The

natural gem has tremendous value because of its scarcity. But to the person who simply wants a ruby for personal adornment because of its rich color and brilliance, the synthetic might be perfectly suitable, and should not be downgraded because of its low cost and ignoble origin.

Books could be filled with information about synthetic and imitation gems. Glassmaking alone is a major industry with a well-developed technology. Only a few synthetic gem materials are usually encountered by the typical gem buyer. The history of their manufacture and a comparison with their natural counterparts can be briefly summarized.

Synthetic Diamond

Diamond and graphite are both pure carbon. The hardness and optical properties of diamond are due to its compact, tightly bonded structure of carbon atoms. This structural arrangement and the occurrence of diamond suggests that it forms in nature under conditions of high temperature and pressure. Early attempts at diamond synthesis were based on this observation.

Many scientists tried to make diamond in the laboratory, among them J. B. Hannay of Glasgow as early as 1880, and Henri Moissan in 1896. Moissan claimed to have succeeded, but his results have never been verified. Diamond synthesis remained elusive until 1955. In that year the General Electric Company revealed its process for manufacturing diamonds.

The largest gem diamonds grown by G.E. are about a carat, and stones of about ½ carat in weight have been cut from some of them. These diamonds are as hard and dispersive as natural gems. They are true diamonds, not imitations. But the cost of manufacture is so high that even in these small sizes synthetic diamond cannot compete with natural diamond on the gem market. This situation might easily change with new technological developments.

 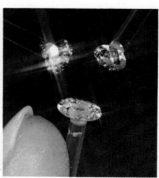

135

G.E. process employs large high-temperature press (opp.).
Synthetic diamond crystals up to one carat in weight have been made
(above l.) that have yielded cut gems up to ½ carat (above r.)

Synthetic Ruby and Sapphire

Ruby and sapphire have long been considered two of the most desired and valuable gems. Natural material has never been available in sufficient quantity to meet world demand. It is therefore not surprising that their synthesis would be considered a worthy goal. The earliest experiments were those of Marc Gaudin in France in the mid-19th Century, although gem quality corundum was not produced. In the mid 1880's, however, rubies appeared on the gem market that were initially thought to be natural, but which careful study showed to be manufactured products. Many of these rubies, known as "Geneva rubies," because it was thought that they were made near Geneva, Switzerland, were sold as natural. Just after the turn of the century another type of ruby appeared on the market. Termed "reconstructed ruby," this material was supposed to have been made by melting together bits of natural ruby. In recent years it has been demonstrated that such a process will not work, so these rubies must also have been synthesized from chemical raw materials.

A commercial process for manufacturing ruby was developed by Edmund Frémy of Paris. His rubies, however, were all in the form of thin plates. They could be manufactured cheaply in great quantity, and were sold widely for use in watch and instrument bearings. But they were too thin to provide large gems of fine color.

In the last decade of the 19th Century, one of Frémy's assistants,

Man-made ruby is usually finer in color and transparency than natural material from North Carolina (above). The flux technique produces ruby crystals (opp.) of fine color.

August Verneuil, developed a new and different technique for synthesizing ruby. Frémy's method involved dissolving aluminum oxide in a molten salt, and allowing ruby to crystallize from the melt by slow cooling. Verneuil's method, which he called "flame fusion," employs the direct melting of aluminum oxide in a flame. The powdered chemical is allowed to dribble from a hopper through a very hot flame. The powder melts in the flame and falls in the form of tiny droplets onto a rotating ceramic rod. Eventually a mass of material builds up which cools and crystallizes as a large single crystal. Ruby can be made by adding a pinch of chromium to the aluminum oxide. Sapphire in various colors requires different combinations of metal oxides. It is interesting that the basic design of the Verneuil furnace hasn't changed much since the day it was first introduced in 1904.

Most synthetic gem ruby and sapphire today is grown by the Verneuil process. The furnaces can be automated so a minimum of personnel can run many machines. Factories in Germany, France, and Switzerland may contain nearly 1,000 furnaces running at the same time, night and day. The output of such factories is measured in tons, rather than carats, and the cost of rough synthetic corundum can be as low as a few cents per carat. The crystals produced, called boules, are cut in mass-production shops, sometimes by machine, or by hand where labor is inexpensive.

A few companies use other techniques for manufacturing corundum. Ruby for lasers is grown by pulling crystals from a melt, in a way reminiscent of pulling taffy, although the procedure is complex and **137**

carefully controlled. A more refined version of Frémy's method is also used to a limited extent. Today the method is called flux fusion, and the process yields ruby of fine color and clarity, although it is far more expensive than the Verneuil process.

Synthetic sapphire and ruby appear in a variety of commercial jewelry, such as class rings and birthstone jewelry. Usually a ring sold as "alexandrite" or "amethyst," where the label includes the quotes, is a synthetic stone. The so-called "alexandrite" sold to tourists throughout the world for a few dollars per stone is a specially made corundum that has a color change reminiscent of true alexandrite. Colorless corundum, or "white sapphire" is manufactured in huge quantities for use as

138

Verneuil process makes ruby and other materials by a stepwise accretion process (top). Hydrothermal ruby (btm.) is not suitable for gem use, although good crystals can be produced.

colorless gems and for bearings in electric meters, as well as for use in specialized electronic applications.

Star ruby and sapphire can be made by adding titanium oxide to the feed powder in a Verneuil furnace. As the corundum cools, the titanium oxide forms crystals of the mineral rutile within the host corundum. The rutile crystals are needle-like and orient themselves according to the symmetry of the corundum, which is hexagonal (six-sided). This produces a six-rayed star when such boules are cut. The color range of synthetic star corundum is the same as that of the faceted gems.

Synthetic corundum has distinguishing characteristics. The Verneuil process always produces curved growth lines which are visible under magnification and with the correct illumination. No natural mineral ever displays such curved lines, called striae, and their presence is a guarantee of synthetic origin. Another characteristic of synthetics is the presence of perfectly round bubbles, sometimes with a small tail like a tadpole. Flux-grown rubies may show characteristic inclusions of the flux. Other tests normally used in gem identification may not be helpful.

Colors of Transparent Synthetic Corundum			
Color	Tradename	Color	Tradename
Colorless	White sapphire	Yellow-brown	Madeira topaz
Red	Ruby	Brown	Palmyra topaz
Dark Red	Garnet	Green	Green sapphire
Deep Pink	Pink sapphire	Pale green	Amaryl
Lilac-Pink	Rose de France	Blue	Burma sapphire
Orange	Padparadscha	Purple	Amethyst
Yellow	Topaz	Purple-green	Alexandrite

Synthetic Spinel

The first synthetic spinel was produced accidentally when some magnesium oxide was added to the feed powder in making synthetic Verneuil corundum. Spinel was not considered an especially valuable gem, however, so more than 20 years passed before synthetic spinel was used commercially in quantity. Natural spinels are not commonly encountered in the gem trade, but synthetic spinels are seen almost everywhere. These gems are widely used to imitate other gems that are considered more desirable, such as emerald, aquamarine, and tourmaline. Synthetic spinel is normally made by the Verneuil process, and boules in a tremendous variety of rich colors can be grown. These colors are due to the addition of chemical impurities because pure spinel, as with pure sapphire, is colorless. In addition, spinel powder mixed with cobalt **139**

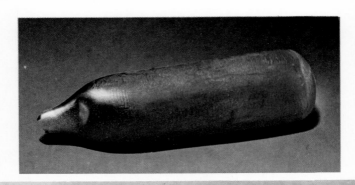

oxide and fused in an electric furnace produces a dense, deep-blue material that strongly resembles lapis lazuli. A spinel that resembles moonstone was introduced in 1957. Some spinel has also been made by flux fusion, but this material has not been used much as gems.

Colors of Synthetic Spinel			
Color	Tradename	Color	Tradename
Colorless	White spinel	Dark green	Tourmaline
Blue	Hope sapphire	Yellow-green	Peridot
Green-blue	Blue zircon	Pink	Pink spinel; kunzite
Pale blue	Aquamarine		
Yellowish-green	Brazilian emerald	Purple	Amethyst
		Green-red	Alexandrite

Synthetic spinels may not show the curved growth lines seen in synthetic Verneuil corundum. But they *can* be identified as spinel, and the colors of the synthetic gems are usually sufficiently different from those of natural spinels to make identification possible.

Synthetic Quartz

Natural quartz is common and inexpensive. Yet synthetic quartz can be made in sufficient quantity and at low enough cost to make gem quartz manufacture worthwhile.

Citrine, or yellow quartz, is colored by iron. Amethyst is made by adding specific impurities that do not produce a visible color, but which cause a purple coloration when the quartz is irradiated by a radioactive source. Colorless quartz is made in ton quantities for use in electronic applications, but is seldom cut as a gem. Green quartz is also manufactured in limited quantity.

Quartz is synthesized by the so-called *hydrothermal process*. This is the way most natural mineral crystals form, in veins and cavities within the earth. The process is basically the deposition of material from **141**

Synthetic spinel (opp. top) is grown in a wide range of colors (above). Synthetic Verneuil corundum (opp. center) is also grown in many colors, although early crystals (btm.) were small and usually red.

hot-water solutions in which the mineral material is dissolved. Natural solutions are very dilute and mineral crystals may take many years to form. In the laboratory the action is speeded up by dissolving the desired material, in this case chunks of natural quartz, in hot water containing chemical solvents.

Synthetic Beryl

Of the various beryl colors, by far the most valuable is the deep green of emerald. Experiments at emerald synthesis are known as early as 1848, but crystals weighing more than one carat could not be synthesized until 1912. Richard Nacken, who also developed the basic process for quartz synthesis, produced small emerald crystals up to about ²/₅ inch long, using a hydrothermal process similar to that used for quartz. Later German experimenters succeeded in growing small emeralds of fine color which were marketed as "Igmerald" by the I. G. Farbenindustrie conglomerate as early as 1934.

After World War II Carroll Chatham of San Francisco introduced emeralds of large size and fine color. These were the result of research dating back to 1930, and apparently a flux-growth technique.

More recently synthetic emeralds have been manufactured by the Linde Air Products Company, Pierre Gilson of Paris, Zerfass of Germany, and others. The Linde emerald is grown hydrothermally using seed plates of colorless beryl. Gems are cut from the emerald that

142

Synthetic quartz (top) can be manufactured in various colors. Quartz is usually grown by accumulation on a "seed plate" (btm.). Synthetic emerald (opp. l.) and opal (opp. r.) are both grown by Pierre Gilson.

accumulates above or below the seed plate, so large thicknesses are required and are expensive to prepare. Large crystals of superb color are made by Gilson, and clusters of synthetic crystals are frequently offered for sale as jewelry items.

Synthetic emeralds can usually be distinguished from natural gems by the presence of characteristic inclusions. Natural emeralds have specific kinds of inclusions which are often diagnostic of the country or mine of origin. Sometimes present are so-called "three-phase" inclusions consisting of a cavity filled with liquid, within which is a gas bubble and a crystal of sodium chloride or another salt. Synthetic emeralds do not generally display such inclusions, but may contain pieces of flux, or other characteristic internal markings. Detection always requires the use of a microscope and sometimes additional gemological testing instruments.

Other Synthetic Gems

In recent years, Pierre Gilson of Paris has introduced three remarkable synthetic gems: opal, turquoise, and lapis lazuli. It is now known that the color flashes in precious opal are due to the regular accumulation of layers of minute spheres. Gilson has duplicated this process in the laboratory, and his synthetic black and white opal is spectacular and natural looking. Careful tests may be required to distinguish it from natural opal.

Gilson turquoise resembles the finest Persian turquoise. It is extremely uniform in color and texture, and available in cut stones or rough blocks. Under the microscope this turquoise consists of an aggregate of tiny spheres of uniform size, allowing it to be readily distinguished from natural turquoise.

Another recently introduced synthetic gem is alexandrite. This is not corundum with an alexandrite-like color change, but rather a synthetic chrysoberyl with suitable impurities added. The color change is green to red, resembling Russian alexandrite. Cut gems several carats in weight are available, but the cost is high for a synthetic—in the range of synthetic emerald.

Synthetic rutile, titanium oxide, appeared on the market in 1948, under various tradenames. Natural rutile is nearly always opaque or a very dense, deep-red color. Synthetic rutile is made by the Verneuil process in a variety of colors, including brown, yellow, red, and blue. Completely colorless stones could not be made, and always have a tinge

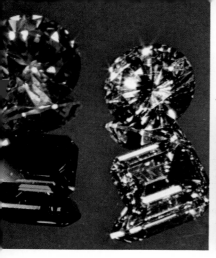

Cut YAG in various colors (l.)
is a substitute for various gems.
Synthetic turquoise (below) by Gilson
resembles Persian material.

of yellow. The colored varieties are seldom seen in the gem trade. Rutile is too soft to be useful as a gemstone (hardness 6–6½ on the Mohs scale). But its dispersion is about six times higher than that of diamond. Cut rutile therefore blazes with myriad colors. The color display is so dazzling and breathtaking that cut rutile loses credibility as the diamond it is supposed to imitate. There is simply too much color to be "real." Cut rutile, often sold as "Titania," is still available, but has lost much of its initial popularity to other, more suitable, diamond imitations.

Some other synthetic materials that have natural analogs include: scheelite (calcium tungstate); apatite (calcium phosphate); wulfenite (lead molybdate); proustite (silver arsenic sulfide); gahnite (zinc aluminate, a variety of spinel); periclase (magnesium oxide); fluorite (calcium fluoride); zincite (zinc oxide); bromellite (beryllium oxide); feldspar (aluminum silicate); zircon (zirconium silicate); phenakite (beryllium silicate); and sphalerite (zinc sulfide). All of these have probably been cut as curiosities for gem collectors.

Diamond Imitations and Others

The appearance of rutile on the market started a hunt for crystals that, when cut, would resemble diamonds. A problem exists with rutile because of its inevitable yellowish color. This problem was solved with the introduction of strontium titanate in 1955. Closely related to rutile, strontium titanate's advantage is its pure white color, with no yellowish tinge. The hardness is, however, 6 on the Mohs scale, still too soft to be very useful in rings. Another advantage of strontium titanate is its dispersion, which, though very high (four times higher than diamond), is lower than that of rutile and thus more realistic. Cut gems do resemble diamonds very strongly, especially when they acquire a slight oily film **145**

Neodymium-fluorapatite (opp. top l.) and erbium-YAG (top r.)
are not available commercially. Plastic and glass imitations (btm.)
are still used extensively in inexpensive jewelry.

which further cuts down the dispersion. Strontium titanate does not exist as a natural mineral. Its softness left an opportunity for a still better diamond imitation material.

This marketing gap was filled by a material called YAG, an acronym for Yttrium Aluminum Garnet. YAG is one of a family of so-called "garnets," named because their internal atomic structure is like that of the natural garnets. But here the similarity ends, because YAG and its brothers with similar rare-earth chemistries, such as GGG (Gadolinium Gallium Garnet), do not occur in nature. YAG was originally grown for use in lasers, which is still its major application. It was accidentally discovered that, when properly cut, YAG strongly resembles cut diamond, even though its dispersion is relatively low. In addition, the hardness of YAG is about 8 on the Mohs scale, so cut gems are durable and do not scratch easily.

YAG can be colored richly by impurities, and cut stones may resemble emerald, kunzite, sapphire, and other gems, although YAG's are too brilliant and hard to be convincing substitutes for most gems.

The newest and most important imitation diamond material is cubic zirconium oxide, or "zirconia." This material is as hard as YAG (8.5), but has a much higher dispersion. In fact, the dispersion of zirconia is slightly higher than that of diamond, giving extremely realistic "fire" to cut gems. Such stones are lively, hard and durable, and virtually indistinguishable from diamond to the untrained eye. Small zirconia gems in jewelry settings will undoubtedly pose severe detection problems for the jewelry trade. Zirconia sells for several tens of dollars per carat, offering the consumer a stone with much of the beauty of diamond at a fraction of the diamond price.

Other gem materials created solely in the laboratory include lithium niobate, sometimes sold as "Linobate," with a Mohs hardness of 6, yttrium aluminate, and potassium tantalate-niobate, whose chemical acronym is KTN. Few cut gems of these materials have appeared on the market, but they would pose a real problem for the average jeweler.

146

Strontium titanate (above) was a better diamond imitation than rutile, but still too soft for use in rings. Doublets of glass and natural gemstones (opp.) are widely used and deceptive.

Doublets and Triplets

Doublets and triplets are composite stones, with either two or three layers. The number of possible combinations of materials usable in making such gems is very large, and a large variety of composites exists in the gem trade.

The normal purpose of a composite stone is to display a good color or present a hard upper surface. Seldom is the bottom portion a genuine stone, although doublets of diamond on sapphire or spinel are known. Commonly seen are doublets with garnet tops and pavilions of glass. The garnet portion is so thin that its color is dominated by the color of the glass, which may be blue, green, pink, red, or blue-green. Colorless doublets are also made. Sometimes a doublet is created with a hollowed-out crown that is filled with liquid and cemented to a color-less base. Frequently seen are doublets with colorless sapphire or spinel crowns and strontium titanate bases. These are effective diamond imita-tions in which the softer titanate provides dispersion color but is pro-tected from wear by a resistant top.

Soudé emeralds are made by cementing together components of colorless quartz, using a green cement to give color to the gem. Such stones are easily detected if unset and viewed from the side. Soudé emeralds are also made using colorless spinel.

Other kinds of doublets include those with quartz top and glass base, or with quartz top and colored-glass base.

Opal doublets consist of slices of opal mounted on a backing of onyx, ceramic, or opal. An opal triplet has an added quartz top. Ingeni-ous jadeite triplets have been made consisting of translucent jadeite top and bottom, but with the upper portion hollowed out and a mass of the same material carefully fitted and cemented in with a rich green-dyed cement. The resulting stone resembles the finest "Imperial" jade. **147**

Altering Gemstone Color

The oldest method of enhancing the color of gems was the use of foil backings. Modern methods are much more subtle and difficult to detect.

The color of opal may be improved by coating the back with a black substance. Occasionally diamonds are "painted" with a pale-colored dye to offset a yellowish tinge, but the coating soon wears off. Quartz is sometimes stained or dyed to resemble jade or tourmaline. Chalcedony is porous and readily absorbs dyes to produce a variety of bright-colored stones. Black onyx is made by soaking grayish-colored chalcedony in a sugar solution and then blackening in sulfuric acid. This process leaves very tiny particles of carbon in the pore spaces of the chalcedony.

There are many ways to improve the color of turquoise, such as by soaking in wax (paraffin) or impregnating with plastics. Such methods are usually detectable, but should generally be suspected if turquoise of deep-blue color is presented at a modest price. Grayish jadeite can be stained to produce an "Imperial" color, or dyed an intense mauve. There is natural mauve jadeite, but the dyed material is much darker in hue. Serpentine, a material not related to jade, can also be stained a rich green color that resembles Imperial jade.

Heating and Irradiation

The effects of heat and irradiation on gems are sometimes unpredictable. In other cases they are used to advantage in improving gem color.

Topaz, for example, occurs in various colors. Pale-blue topaz is not uncommon, but deep, intense blue stones do not occur in nature. Such gems can be produced by gamma-irradiation of certain colorless topaz. This treatment turns the material greenish-brown, but heating produces a rich blue color. Some golden or yellow topaz can be heat-treated to produce a pink or purplish-red color. The color of pale-brown or "sherry"-colored topaz can sometimes be improved by gamma irradiation, but heating or exposure to sunlight usually reverses the process. Color fading of natural brown, sherry, and some blue topaz is not uncommon. Unfortunately, in the case of blue topaz there is no current way to detect color enhancement by gamma irradiation. Although some fading may occur, beyond a certain point the color seems to be stable.

Heating usually lightens the color of tourmaline, but sometimes a dark-green stone can be made an attractive emerald color. Gamma irradiation of tourmaline produces spectacular color changes. Pale-pink and some colorless stones may turn dark pink. Medium-pink material may turn yellow, and blue gems may turn purple. Pale-yellow tourmaline can be made a peach color by gamma rays.

Heating is standard procedure with zircon, turning the drab and unappealing brown and green material into lovely and desirable color-

less and blue gemstones.

Tanzanite coloration has been a subject of intense study. Heating of certain crystals, which eliminates the red-violet color component, produces the lively sapphire-blue color that has made the gem so popular.

Aquamarine of dark-blue color is quite rare and very costly. Many of the dark stones seen in jewelry are produced by heating greenish or brownish material to a temperature of 400–450°C. The treatment results in a permanent color change. A type of beryl known as "Maxixe type" has a distinctive indigo or cobalt-blue color that can be produced by irradiation. Sunlight and heating both bleach the color to yellow or tan, and eventually turn it colorless.

Spodumene is not normally heated, although some yellowish-brown material may be induced to a purplish color by heating. Lilac kunzite can be turned an intense emerald-green by gamma irradiation.

Amethyst may turn brownish or red at a temperature between 400 and 500°C, but sometimes a green color is produced and such gems are sold as "greened amethyst," or "Prasiolite." Further heating causes a complete loss of color. The heating of amethyst to a brownish-yellow color is carried out on a commercial scale. The resulting material is often sold as "Madeira topaz," a misleading name that should be abandoned. A lighter shade has been called "Palmyra topaz," and reddish stones "Spanish topaz." The color change of amethyst due to heating is not always predictable and fading is a possibility.

The most commonly heat-treated gem is quartz. Synthetic amethyst is made from a specially prepared smoky quartz by gamma-ray bombardment. It appears likely that natural amethyst acquires its color in the same manner. Gamma irradiation plus heating of some Brazilian quartz produces a bright greenish-yellow color not found in nature. This color fades substantially in sunlight.

Gamma irradiation of some pearls leads to a gray or bluish-gray color (though not the "black" found in nature). The treatment can be used to improve the color of greenish pearls. The gamma-induced color is uniform and does not fade noticeably in sunlight. **149**

Dyed gems, such as these agate rings (above), are frequently encountered in the gem trade. Some color treatments are difficult to detect, although most are easy to reveal.

Gems as Investments

The dictionary defines an investment as "the outlay of money for income or profit." A good investment must therefore return money to the investor in the form of a continual payment (as with a stock dividend) or the sale of the investment item at a price higher than the purchase price (capital gains).

An ideal investment offers a high yield (rate of return), or the prospect of substantial appreciation, with minimal risk. Usually higher gain potential is achieved with accompanying higher risk. And, to one degree or another, all investments can be considered speculative ventures.

Gems, antiques, art, old cars, stamps, comic books, and other "collectables" do not provide a steady monetary return, like high yield stocks. Their potential as investments is based solely on their ability to appreciate in value. But what is value? It is the attribute given by human beings to things that they wish to gain and/or keep. The idea of "intrinsic value" is almost a contradiction in terms, because only humans can endow value on a commodity through their desire to possess it. Since humans can change their values, all commodities are subject to the status they are given in different societies and cultures, and at different historical times.

Several commodities, however, seem to have found favor in nearly all societies and cultures, in all historical periods. Their value has thus become traditional and a part of human civilization. Their association with concepts of wealth, treasure, desire, status, and power runs like a thread through history. Their value is thus universally accepted and acknowledged throughout the world. These commodities are the precious metals, and gems.

To be sure, specific gems have risen and fallen from favor in specific societies at specific times. Bohemian garnets were all the rage in Victorian times, but are hardly seen today. Amber and lapis were royal gems in ancient cultures, but no longer command kingly prices. But gems *in general* have acquired, through millennia of tradition, the status of "intrinsically" valuable objects, like gold bars. Therefore, while specific gems may not rise appreciably in cost in a given period of years, they are likely to *hold* their value extremely well.

Gems must nevertheless be considered speculative investments. The key to an investment is its liquidity (ease of disposal) and the nature of its ultimate sale, because profit is realized only at this stage. Some gems, such as diamonds and fine, small rubies, emeralds, and sapphires are very easily sold, because the market demand is very large. But how will the owner sell his gem? If he bought it at retail prices, and sells it to a merchant some time later, he may only be paid half of the retail value at

the time of sale. Even if the gem doubled in value in the intervening period, the seller ends up only with the amount he used to purchase the gem. In this case he has lost money, because inflation has diminished the purchasing power of the money he receives. If the seller finds a retail customer himself, however, he might double his money. So the investment potential of a gem depends largely on how it is ultimately converted back into cash.

Another factor is marketability. A very unusual or rare gem may bring a high price. But if the owner wishes to sell his stone, he may find that few people will buy it from him, because its scarcity has prevented the development of a widespread demand. The only buyer might then be another collector, or a connoisseur of fine or rare gemstones. These people do exist, and ultimately may be a significant factor in the gem trade. Thus, the ultimate marketability of rare stones will depend on the ability of gem dealers to make these gems widely known and appreciated.

Some gems have risen dramatically in price in recent years. Tanzanite, for example, virtually unknown in 1965, more than quintupled in price within a decade. This was the result of good marketing to create a demand for the gem. Aquamarine of fine, dark blue color showed similar price appreciation. Other gems also rose substantially in price. An important factor to consider in examining this performance is the saleability of gems, compared to other investment items. Almost every culture uses gems in some way. Gems may play a role in international politics and finance, whereas antiques and art do not, or certainly not to the same degree.

Are gems, then, a good investment? The answer is a qualified yes. The qualifications are: specific type of gem, purchase price, marketability, quality of stone, ultimate disposition, the fashion of the times, and the state of the economy. These factors may dissuade the would-be gem investor, and this is certainly an area where expert advice would be welcome.

151

Tanzanite, blue zoisite from Tanzania,
has displayed price appreciation unrivaled
by other gems in recent years.

Gem Testing

The gemologist must identify gems nondestructively. This limits the available testing methods to optical and physical measurements, rather than scratching or chemical analysis. Some features are so characteristic of particular gems that visual identification can be made with certainty.

Color alone is not a good identification criterion, for it can be misleading. Color merely helps the gemologist limit the range of possible choices. The eye is limited in the detail it can resolve, and inclusions in gems are often diagnostic. A binocular microscope that creates a stereoscopic image is therefore widely used for examining gems. In some cases particular inclusions can indicate the mine from which a gem came. Synthetic gems have characteristic internal features useful in identification. Verneuil-grown synthetics display curved growth lines, never seen in natural gems. Round bubbles are also diagnostic of synthetics or glass.

Refractive index is a useful parameter, usually measured with a device called the refractometer. The eye can judge refractive power to some degree, but cutting disguises this property in many cases.

Specific gravity is an important gem property, usually measured by means of so-called heavy liquids. The specific gravity of a gem is determined by seeing whether it will sink, float up, or remain stationary in a liquid with a known specific gravity.

Fluorescence is diagnostic of many synthetic gems, such as Chatham emeralds and various synthetic rubies. Doublets and glasses may also fluoresce, revealing their origin or manufacturing method.

Pleochroism in gems is detected with devices called the polariscope and the dichroscope. The former instrument also measures double refraction. These devices are simply constructed from sheets of polarizing material such as are found in sunglasses.

The spectroscope is useful in identification, because it reveals the so-called absorption spectrum of a gem.

Other gem-testing tools include solvents for removing coatings and dyes, a hot-needle for testing amber and turquoise, dilute acids, and a simple magnet.

Erbium-YAG (above l.) is an exotic gem. Its fluorescence (r.) is strong and diagnostic. Gem hobbyists who attend club-sponsored shows often find tables (opp.) heaped with cutting material for their selection.

Lapidary Hobby

Lapidary, the art of gem cutting, is one of the fastest-growing hobbies in the world. In the United States some hobby magazines have paid circulations numbering tens of thousands. Dozens of books have been published on all aspects of the lapidary craft, covering everything from grinding cabochons to setting gems in handmade jewelry.

In the United States mineral and gem clubs are present in nearly all major cities. A large percentage of these clubs are organized in a Federation System, with various regional Federations affiliated together as the AFMS, American Federation of Mineralogical Societies, which celebrated its 25th Anniversary in 1972. The member clubs have many activities, including field trips, sponsored lectures, tours, auctions, special exhibits and community programs, and swapping sessions. Some clubs have sufficient resources to host shows, where invited dealers sell their wares at booths. Such shows are major local events and offer the gem enthusiast an opportunity to see many cut stones, usually at prices lower than those charged in retail shops. The Lapidary Journal contains in every issue a major calendar listing local shows throughout the United States and Canada.

Mineral and gem shows are also places to see lapidary equipment, rough material, supplies, books, and hobby accessories and tools. At many shows there are demonstrations of specific techniques, such as carving or faceting. In addition there are usually many different kinds of exhibits, including minerals, gems, fossils, educational displays, and specialty crafts. The April issue of the Lapidary Journal also lists most of the clubs in the United States and Canada, including the name of the secretary, address, and where and when the club meets.

Jewelry Metals

Jewelry metals include silver, gold, platinum, and a few other rare elements; this group as a whole consists of the so-called "precious metals."

Pure gold is 24 karat; the karat designation is a measure of "fineness." By law, gold jewelry must be stamped if above 10 karat; gold less than 10K fine *cannot* have a karat mark or be called "gold." Gold-filled and plated articles consist of a metal base covered with a thin sheet of gold at least 10K fine. Gold-filled articles must be at least 1/20 by weight of gold of the quality stated, such as "1/20 12K gold filled." Colored gold is produced by alloying: copper (red), cadmium and silver (green), iron (blue), nickel or palladium (white), and aluminum or zinc (purple).

Pure silver is taken to mean 99.99 percent silver. Most so-called "pure" silver available is less than 99.5 percent or "995 fine." Sterling silver is not less than 925 fine, or 92.5 percent silver. Coin silver is generally 900 fine, and articles less than 900 fine *cannot*, by law, be

represented as "silver." Federal law prohibits the use of the terms "Sterling" or "coin" on plated articles.

Platinum and related metals (iridium, rhodium, osmium, palladium, and ruthenium) are used extensively in jewelry. Platinum is harder than gold and therefore more difficult to work, but better for securely holding fine gems in settings. Platinum metal alloys are designated according to composition, such as 0.600 Plat., 0.350 Pall., indicating 60 percent platinum, 35 percent palladium, and 5 percent of some other metal.

Silver tends to tarnish with time, due to the formation of a black oxide coating. This can be polished off, but can be prevented entirely by plating a silver article with rhodium, which is bright and silvery but will not tarnish. This plating does not affect the value of the article.

A hallmark is a stamp applied by an organization to indicate the fineness of a precious metal article. Such marks are applied only after **154** assay proves that the metal meets the required standards.

Silver (l.) and gold (r.) are the most desirable of all metals, and have retained their image of value for thousands of years.

Popular Styles of Cutting

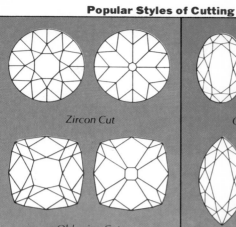

Zircon Cut

Oval Cut

Old-mine Cut

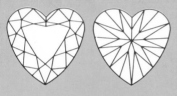

Marquise Cut

Heart-shaped Brilliant Cut

Emerald Cut

French Cut

Table Cut

Square Cut

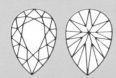

Pear-shaped Cut

Baguette Cut

Tapered Baguette

Birthstones

Month	Natural Stone	Synthetic Stone
January	Garnet	Synthetic corundum
February	Amethyst	Synthetic corundum
March	Aquamarine or Bloodstone	Synthetic spinel
April	Diamond	Synthetic spinel
May	Emerald	Synthetic spinel or emerald
June	Pearl, moonstone, or alexandrite	Cultured pearl or synthetic corundum
July	Ruby	Synthetic ruby
August	Peridot or sardonyx	Synthetic spinel
September	Sapphire	Synthetic sapphire
October	Opal or pink tourmaline	Synthetic corundum
November	Topaz or citrine	Synthetic corundum
December	Turquoise or zircon	Synthetic spinel

Magazines:
THE LAPIDARY JOURNAL, *P.O. Box 80937, San Diego, California 92138*
GEMS AND MINERALS, *P.O. Box 687, Mentone, California 92359*
ROCK AND GEM, *1600 Ventura Blvd., Encino, California 91346*
ROCKHOUND, *P.O. Box 328, Conroe, Texas 77301*

Books:
THE GEM KINGDOM, *by Paul E. Desautels.*
    Ridge Press—Random House, New York, 1970
GEMS, *by Robert Webster. Butterworths,*
    London, 1970
PRECIOUS STONES, *by Max Bauer.*
    Dover Publications, New York, 1968,
    2 volumes (paperback, originally published 1904)
GEMSTONES, *by G. F. Herbert Smith.*
    Pitman Publishing Corp., New York, 1958
HANDBOOK OF GEM IDENTIFICATION, *by Richard T. Liddicoat, Jr.*
    Gemological Institute of America, Los Angeles, 1972
VAN NOSTRAND'S STANDARD CATALOG OF GEMS, *by John Sinkankas.*
    D. Van Nostrand Co., Inc., Princeton, 1968

For additional information on commercial and rare gems,
gem cleaners, sources of gems and identification services, contact author at
P.O. Box 996, Laytonsville, MD 20760.

Index

159

Joel E. Arem is a Ph.D. mineralogist, author, photographer, lecturer, and former curator at the Smithsonian Institution. He is the President of Multifacet, Inc., a diversified company specializing in gems, precious metals, and consulting services in the area of "real-value" commodities and investments.